MOHANDAS K. GANDHI

MOHANDAS K. GANDHI

Charles J. Shields

1348)

Introduction by James Scott Brady,
Trustee, the Center to Prevent Handgun Violence
Vice Chairman, the Brain Injury Foundation

Chelsea House Publishers

Philadelphia

Frontispiece: Gandhi reads his correspondence, 1924.

CHELSEA HOUSE PUBLISHERS

EDITOR IN CHIEF Sally Cheney
DIRECTOR OF PRODUCTION Kim Shinners
PRODUCTION MANAGER Pamela Loos
ART DIRECTOR Sara Davis
COVER PHOTO Hulton/Archive Photos
LAYOUT 21st Century Publishing and Communications, Inc.

First Printing

1 3 5 7 9 8 6 4 2

The Chelsea House World Wide Web address is
http://www.chelseahouse.com

Library of Congress Cataloging-in-Publication Data

Shields, Charles.
Mohandas K. Gandhi / Charles Shields
    p.   cm. — (Overcoming adversity)
Includes bibliographical references and index.
ISBN 0-7910-6301-1 (alk. paper)
1. Gandhi, Mahatma, 1869–1948—Juvenile literature. 2. Statesmen—India—
Biography—Juvenile literature. 3. Nationalists—India—Biography—Juvenile
literature. [1. Gandhi, Mahatma, 1869–1948. 2. Statesmen. 3. India—Politics
and government—1919–1947.] I. Title. II. Series.

DS481.G3 S4868 2001
954.03'5'092—dc21
[B]
                                                                   2001028678

22.95/ 18.36 Baker + taylor 12/02

CONTENTS

OVERCOMING ADVERSITY

ON FACING ADVERSITY

James Scott Brady

I GUESS IT'S a long way from a Centralia, Illinois, train yard to the George Washington University Hospital Trauma Unit. My dad was a yardmaster for the old Chicago, Burlington & Quincy Railroad. As a child, I used to get to sit in the engineer's lap and imagine what it was like to drive that train. I guess I always have liked being in the "driver's seat."

Years later, however, my interest turned from driving trains to driving campaigns. In 1979, former Texas governor John Connally hired me as a press secretary in his campaign for the American presidency. We lost the Republican primary to a former Hollywood star named Ronald Reagan. But I managed to jump over to the Reagan campaign. When Reagan was elected in 1980, I was "sitting in the catbird seat," as humorist James Thurber would say—poised to be named presidential press secretary. I held that title throughout the eight years of the Reagan administration. But not without one terrible, extended interruption.

It happened barely two months after the Reagan administration took office. I never even heard the shots. On March 30, 1981, my life went blank in an instant. In an attempt to assassinate President Reagan, John Hinckley Jr. armed himself with a "Saturday night special"—a low-quality, $29 pistol—and shot wildly as our presidential entourage exited a Washington hotel. One of the exploding bullets struck me just above the left eye. It shattered into a couple dozen fragments, some of which penetrated my skull and entered my brain.

The next few months of my life were a nightmare of repeated surgery, broken contact with the outside world, and a variety of medical complications. More than once, I was very close to death.

The next few years were filled with frustrating struggles to function with a paralyzed right side, struggles to speak and communicate.

To people who face and defeat daunting obstacles, "ambition" is not becoming wealthy or famous or winning elections or awards. Words like "ambition" and "achievement" and "success" take on very different meanings. The objective is just to live, to wake up every morning. The goals are not lofty; they are very ordinary.

My own heroes are ordinary folks—but they accomplish extraordinary things because they try. My greatest hero is my wife, Sarah. She's accomplished a lot of things in life, but two stand out. The first has been the way she has cared for me and our son since I was shot. A tremendous tragedy and burden was dropped unexpectedly into her life, totally beyond her control and without justification. She could have given up; instead, she focused her energies on preserving our family and returning our lives to normal as much as possible. Week by week, month by month, year by year, she has not reached for the miraculous, just for the normal. Yet in focusing on the normal, she has helped accomplish the miraculous.

Her other most remarkable accomplishment, to me, has been spearheading the effort to keep guns out of the hands of criminals and children in America. Opponents call her a "gun grabber"; I call her a national hero. And I am not alone.

After a seven-year battle, during which Sarah and I worked tirelessly to educate the public about the need for stronger gun laws, the Brady Bill became law in 1993. It was a victory, achieved in the face of tremendous opposition, that now benefits all Americans. From the time the law took effect through fall 1997, background checks had stopped 173,000 criminals and other high-risk purchasers from buying handguns, and the law has helped to reduce illegal gun trafficking.

Sarah was not pursuing fame, or even recognition. She simply started at one point—when our son, Scott, found a loaded handgun on the seat of a pickup truck and, thinking it was a toy, pointed it at Sarah.

Fortunately, no one was hurt. But seeing a gun nearly bring a second tragedy upon our family, Sarah became determined to do whatever she could to prevent senseless death and injury from guns.

Some people think of Sarah as a powerful political force. To me, she's the person who so many times fed me and helped me dress during my long years of recovery.

Overcoming obstacles is part of life, not just for people who are challenged by disabilities, illnesses, or tragedies, but for all people. No matter what the obstacle—fear, disability, prejudice, grief, or a difficulty that isn't likely to "just go away"—we can all work to make this world a better place.

Mahatma Gandhi walks with his granddaughter Manu. As the two, along with another granddaughter, made their way down a path from Gandhi's residence to prayer grounds, an assassin would pull Manu out of the way and fatally shoot India's revered spiritual leader.

1

"THE LIGHT HAS GONE OUT"

ON THE EVENING of January 30, 1948, millions of people in India and Pakistan listened in disbelief to an announcement on All-India Radio by Jawaharlal Nehru, India's prime minister. "Friends and comrades," Nehru declared, "the light has gone out of our lives and there is darkness everywhere. I do not know what to tell you and how to say it. Our beloved leader, Bapu as we call him, the Father of the Nation, is no more. . . . A madman has put an end to his life."

"Over all India," the Associated Press reported, "the word spread like wildfire. Minutes after the flash was received in Bombay, rioting broke out, with Hindu extremists attacking Moslems. A panic-stricken Moslem woman echoed the thoughts of thousands with a cry: " 'God help us all!' "

Bapu, or Father, was the affectionate nickname for Mohandas K. Gandhi, a former lawyer turned political activist. For more than 30 years, Gandhi had waged a campaign of nonviolence against the colonial British government in India. In August 1947, six months before his assassination, India had finally gained its independence.

"All this has happened when there was so much more for him to do," Prime Minister Nehru continued in his broadcast. "We could never think that he was unnecessary or that he had done his task. But now, particularly when we are faced with so many difficulties, his not being with us is a blow most terrible to bear."

Earlier that day, the 79-year-old Gandhi had sat for a light meal in the late afternoon with friends in his room at Birla House in New Delhi. A Hindu vegetarian all his life, he ate from a plate of cooked vegetables and oranges, spiced with a sauce made from ginger, lemon juice, and aloe, and listened to Sardar Vallabhbhai Patel, deputy prime minister, explain the latest political developments.

Gandhi had begun eating regularly again only recently. Two weeks earlier, when renewed fighting broke out between Hindus and Moslems (today followers of the Islamic faith are generally called Muslims), he had pledged to go without food until it stopped. So powerful was his influence over the hearts and minds of millions in India, that peace returned within five days.

During his meal, he chatted with Patel and Patel's daughter and secretary, Maniben, until Abha Gandhi, the young wife of a relative, interrupted. Knowing how Gandhi hated being late, Abha showed him the time on his nickel-plated watch. It was close to 5 P.M., when he normally attended a daily prayer service on the grounds outside. Nearly 1,000 admirers were already assembled for the service, waiting to catch a glimpse of him.

"I must tear myself away," he said to his guests, and rose to go outside.

He was frail from age and years of self-imposed hardship. During his life, he had walked thousands of miles from village to village, preaching and advising the listening crowds about the nonviolent path to independence for his country. He had spent long periods in prison on charges of lawbreaking. In sympathy with the poor, he preferred wearing a white, sacklike *dhoti*, or robe, in all weather, and he maintained a simple diet. Now, as he entered the garden surrounding his residence and started down the path toward the prayer grounds, he leaned his thin forearms for support on the shoulders of Abha and his granddaughter, Manu Gandhi. "My walking sticks," he liked to call them.

As they traveled through the red-stone colonnade leading to the little pagoda set aside for prayer services, Gandhi began to tease his two helpers about the carrot juice Abha had given him to drink earlier.

"So," he said, "you're giving me cattle food!"

"Ba used to call it 'horse food,'" Abha replied. Ba was Gandhi's late wife, Kasturbai (her name is also frequently spelled Kasturba).

"Isn't it grand of me," Gandhi said, pretending to be pleased with himself, "to enjoy what no one else wants?"

"Bapu, your watch must be feeling very neglected," said Abha, changing the subject. "You would not look at it today."

"Why should I, since you are my timekeepers?"

By now they were crossing the grass through an enormous crowd that parted to clear a path for them. Gandhi walked up the stairs leading to the level ground where he would sit on a wooden platform for the service.

"I am late by 10 minutes," Gandhi chided himself aloud. "I hate being late. I should have been here at the stroke of five." He paused to press his hands together in the traditional Hindu greeting to everyone.

From the crowd, a few people surged forward to bow at his feet. One of them was 37-year-old Nathuram Godse, well educated and, in his words, "intensely proud of Hinduism as a whole." Godse was a Hindu nationalist who believed that India should be a completely Hindu nation—in culture, values, and faith. He was incensed by what he believed was Gandhi's betrayal of that ideal.

Gandhi constantly preached tolerance for Moslems, Sikhs, and other non-Hindus. Worse, he had allowed himself to be forced into accepting the creation of an independent Pakistan for India's Moslems, carved out of India's northern territory.

To Godse, these actions were unforgivable. Moreover, he had nothing but contempt for Gandhi's belief that nonviolence could bring about change. "I could never conceive that an armed resistance to an aggression is unjust. I would consider it a religious and moral duty to resist and, if possible, to overpower such an enemy by use of force," he later read aloud from a prepared statement at his trial. He decided that the only way to stop Gandhi's influence was to kill him. "I sat brooding intensely on the atrocities perpetrated on Hinduism and its dark and deadly future if left to face Islam outside and Gandhi inside, and . . . I decided all of a sudden to take the extreme step against Gandhi," he later said.

Godse's first assassination attempt had occurred 10 days earlier, on January 20. During the prayer service at Birla House that day, Godse and several other conspirators, including his brother Gopal, detonated a bomb in the garden wall. They hoped the explosion would draw the crowd away from Gandhi. But when it didn't, they stopped short of tossing a grenade at their intended victim for fear of killing bystanders.

This time, however, Godse relied on a simpler plan. Roughly, he pushed aside people until he blocked Gandhi's way. When Manu stepped forward and took hold of Godse's hand, trying to lead him out of their path because they were late, he wrenched her aside. She stumbled. Quickly he knelt, as if to show respect to Gandhi, but instead pulled a nine-shot automatic pistol from his khaki jacket pocket. To the crowd, the three shots sounded like firecrackers.

"He, Rama [Oh, God]," Gandhi murmured. He "crumpled instantly," according to news reports, "putting his hand

Nathuram Godse murdered Gandhi, a fellow Hindu, because Gandhi preached peaceful coexistence with India's Moslems.

to his forehead in the Hindu gesture of forgiveness to his assassin. Three bullets penetrated his body at close range. One in the upper right thigh, one in the abdomen, and one in the chest."

The crowd instantly descended on Godse, but police guards used rifles and bayonets to force them back until the assassin could be hustled off under arrest. Several people lifted Gandhi, his eyes half-closed, and carried him into Birla House. Sardar Patel, the deputy minister,

Prime Minister Jawaharlal Nehru eulogizes his country's preeminent leader. Gandhi, he said, "represented something more than the immediate present; [he] represented the living, the eternal truths, reminding us of the right path, drawing us from error, taking this ancient country to freedom."

felt for Gandhi's pulse and thought he detected a faint one. Someone rummaged through a medicine chest looking for anything that might be useful. By the time a doctor arrived a few minutes later, however, Gandhi was dead.

His watch, which had fallen to the ground, had stopped at 5:12 P.M.

"The light has gone out, I said, and yet I was wrong,"

said Prime Minister Nehru later that evening during his radio broadcast. "For the light that shone in our country was no ordinary light. The light that has illumined this country for these many, many years will illumine this country for many more years, and a thousand years later that light will still be seen in this country and the world will see it and it will give solace to innumerable hearts. For that light represented something more than the immediate present; it represented the living, the eternal truths, reminding us of the right path, drawing us from error, taking this ancient country to freedom."

Mohandas K. Gandhi (right) and his older brother Laxmidas, 1886. The Gandhis, members of the Vaisya caste of bankers and tradespeople, lived comfortably.

2

GANDHI'S CHILDHOOD

THE INDIA INTO which Mohandas Gandhi was born on October 2, 1869, was like a giant in handcuffs and chains. Resentment against the British had been welling up for generations. British land reforms had reduced the size of many farms in India, and colonial land taxes had forced farmers deep into poverty. British influence over the economy was so powerful that when England imported cheaper machine-made mill cloth to India, it completely destroyed the country's hand-loom cloth industry. Millions in India starved. Lord Bentinck, the governor-general of India, reported to the British government in 1834: "The bones of the cotton weavers are bleaching the plains of India."

In 1857, that resentment boiled over into the Indian Rebellion. It started at an army base in Meerut, near Delhi, where British officers ordered Indian soldiers, called *sepoys,* to bite open gunpowder cartridges to load their rifles. It was rumored that the grease on the cartridges was made of cow and hog fat. Religious beliefs forbade the Hindu sepoys from eating beef, and Moslem sepoys could not eat pork. They refused to obey, interpreting it as further proof that Britain meant to ruin India, this time by violating the people's religious beliefs.

Violence broke out on May 10 when an Indian soldier shot his British commander rather than obey the order. Some Indian leaders, seizing on the fact that the army of 300,000 was 96 percent Indian, called for an uprising against British rule.

The rebellion spread so rapidly from Meerut into northern and central India that authorities struggled hard to suppress it. Fortunately for the British, some Indian states avoided the rebellion altogether. In addition, army commanders relied heavily on disciplined Sikh soldiers of the Punjab region to fight the mutineers. In the end, the rebels' poor leadership and lack of weapons led to their defeat in 1859.

Nevertheless, the British had suffered their first serious challenge to colonial rule in India, and the lesson was not wasted. It was clear that Britain could not afford to take for granted its control over a country that, after China, had the world's second largest population.

In the 150 years before the Indian Rebellion, the British had come to dominate India by default. Since the mid-1700s, the only real power in India had been the British East India Trading Company. Slowly it changed from a mere import-export business chartered by Queen Elizabeth I in 1600, to a foreign conqueror that replaced the crumbling Mughal Empire. At the Battle of Plassey in 1757, the forces of Robert Clive, an agent of the East India Company, defeated the army of the *nawab* (Mughal governor) of Bengal. Most historians consider the outcome of that battle the start of the British Empire in India. In 1774, Parliament appointed Warren Hastings as the British East India Trading Company's first governor-general of India.

But the Indian Rebellion—or Sepoy Mutiny, as it was also called—radically changed how Britain ruled its vast, troublesome Eastern conquest. In 1858, in the midst of the rebellion, the British government moved to govern

India directly. Parliament took control of the East India Company's Indian possessions, which collectively became known as British India. British rule in India was also often called the Raj (from a word meaning rule or administration). In other parts of India—called the princely or native states—the British governed indirectly through local rulers. And a few small areas of coastal land remained French or Portuguese colonies until the mid-1900s.

The British monarch, Queen Victoria, appointed a viceroy to govern British India. An executive council of five members—all British and all appointed by the queen—helped the viceroy govern. The viceroy, in turn, appointed from 6 to 12 additional members, who met with the executive council to form a legislative council. A few Indians could serve on the legislative council, but clearly the system was designed to keep the reins of political power firmly in British hands.

With the help of elephants, rebel Indian soldiers transport cannons to be used in the siege of Delhi, 1857. Though the British quashed the Indian Rebellion—also called the Sepoy Mutiny—after two years of fighting, resentment of colonial rule continued to simmer.

British India was further divided into several provinces. An appointed governor or lieutenant governor headed each province. The provinces also had their own executive and legislative councils. Finally, as if to put the royal seal on the entire map of India, in 1876 Parliament gave Queen Victoria the title empress of India.

To their credit, the British did much to improve India in the second half of the 19th century. They built railroad, telegraph, and telephone systems. They also established universities, although little money was spent on elementary education. In addition, the British enlarged the Indian irrigation system, but agricultural production improved only slightly. Industrialization, which had begun improving the standard of living in Europe almost 150 years earlier, was practically unknown in India. In general, India under the British remained strictly administered, but hopelessly poor.

Into this stew of Western and Eastern politics, religion, and economics, Mohandas Karamchand Gandhi was born in 1869 in Porbandar, India, located on the west coast of the small principality of Gujart. The name "Gandhi" means "grocer," although the family was involved in local government. Mohandas was born into the Vaisya caste, a social class composed of bankers and tradespeople. In India, a person's caste—and thus to a large extent the course of his or her life—is determined by birth. Within a caste, most people share the same culture or occupation, belong to the same religious sect (group), and enjoy the same level of wealth. Each caste has its own customs and rituals. To maintain ritual purity, members of each caste neither marry nor even dine with members of other castes.

The first, or top-ranked, caste belonged to the Brahmans, or religious leaders. Second was the Kshatriyas—rulers, nobles, and warriors. Then came the Vaisyas, to which Gandhi's family belonged, and finally the Sudras, composed of artisans and laborers. A fifth category was outside the caste system altogether. This was the *panchamas*, or "untouchables." Untouchables performed work believed unfit for anyone else. Although in his lifetime Gandhi fought to abolish the low status and shame heaped on the untouchables, about one-fifth of India's population today still falls into this category.

When Mohandas was about seven, his father, Karamchand Gandhi, became the *dewan*, or prime minister of the principality of Rajkot. He was skillful at negotiating deals between Rajkot's princes and the rather heavy-handed British officials. In Gandhi's autobiography, *My Experiments with Truth*, he described his father as "a lover of his clan, truthful, brave and generous, but short-tempered."

Karamchand Gandhi married four times—the last when he was over 40—each time after his previous wife died. Mohandas was the youngest of his father's six children, but he would fault his father for marrying his mother, the fourth wife, because "[t]o a certain extent he might have been even given to carnal pleasures." In other words, Gandhi believed his father was at an age when he should have put sex aside. That's what Gandhi did, in fact, in his own marriage while still in his thirties.

Gandhi's mother, Putlibai, was a deeply religious woman who divided her time between her duties as a wife and mother and her duties to the temple. The Gandhi household was devoted to Vaishnavism, a sect of Hinduism, and Mohandas attended temple regularly. His mother made fasting, or going without eating, a way to express her faith. Gandhi recalled his mother fasting two or three days straight and it "was nothing to her." Besides the impression that his mother's fasting made on him—Gandhi would later use fasting as a tool in his own leadership—the Gandhi family also respected the religious practices of Jainism. Jainism preaches nonviolence and the belief that each thing in the universe is eternal. As he grew older, Gandhi adapted some of the values of Jainism—tolerance for others, vegetarianism, and fasting for self-improvement—to his own commitment as a Hindu to *ahimsa*, which vows not to harm other living things.

This 1876 photo, the oldest known image of Mohandas Gandhi, shows him as a boy of seven.

In fact, practicing the right behavior seems to have absorbed Gandhi even as a little boy. In his autobiography, he recalled reading a child's story about Shravana, who carried his old and blind parents in two baskets slung on a bamboo yoke. He was so touched by the story that he vowed to be like Shravana and serve his parents too. About the same time, he attended a play about a fairy-tale king named Harishchandra, who suffered because he defended the truth. "'Why should not all be truthful like Harishchandra?' was the question I asked myself day and night," Gandhi recalled. "To follow truth and to go through all the ordeals

Harishchandra went through was the one ideal it inspired in me."

Sometimes his childish thoughts about evil tormented him. He was afraid of darkness, ghosts, thieves, and snakes. Noticing this, a maidservant in the house suggested he ask for Rama's (God's) help when he felt afraid. Gandhi took to repeating "Rama" to himself when something fearful bothered him.

School seems not to have interested Gandhi much, perhaps because there were so few resources for children. He and his classmates wrote their letters in the dust. His report card ranked him as "good at English, fair in Arithmetic, and weak in Geography; conduct very good, bad handwriting."

"He did not shine in the classroom," wrote one of his biographers, "or in the playground. Quiet, shy and retiring, he was tongue-tied in company. He did not mind being rated as a mediocre student, but he was exceedingly jealous of his reputation. He was proud of the fact that he had never told a lie to his teachers or classmates." In fact, the only memory Gandhi described about school involved refusing to cheat. During a visit by a school inspector, Gandhi misspelled the word *kettle*. The teacher, recalled Gandhi, hinted that he should hurry up and copy the word from another student. "But I would not be prompted," he said. "It was beyond me to see that he wanted me to copy the spelling from my neighbor's slate, for I had thought the teacher was there to supervise us against copying. . . . I could never learn the art of 'copying.'"

Still, like most young people, Mohandas could not resist rebelling sometimes. A friend persuaded him that the British ruled India "because they eat meat. If we become meat-eaters, like them, we will be able to drive them out." Although his religious faith restricted him to a vegetarian diet, Gandhi secretly tried eating meat away from home. Afterward, he felt so guilty he promised never to do it again. Another time, his conscience got the best of him when he stole one of his brother's gold bracelets to purchase cigarettes. Ashamed, he wrote a confession to his father. His father read the letter and then sadly tore it up, apparently too hurt to say anything. Gandhi felt even more remorse.

As young and unsure as he was, however, the society in which Gandhi lived did not think he was too young to marry. At 13, he became the husband—though in his autobiography he sarcastically called it "playing the husband"—of a girl the same age, named Kasturbai. Gandhi did not say how the two of them met, although he implies their parents arranged the marriage. The reason he was only 13 at the time of his marriage, he explained somewhat bitterly, was that his family wanted to have a triple wedding involving his older brother and a cousin. In his autobiography he skipped over the ceremony, noting only that his father was injured in an accident on the way to the wedding, from which the older man never completely recovered. He died three years later. "However, I forgot my grief over my father's injuries in the childish amusement of the wedding," Gandhi confessed, again emphasizing his immaturity.

In photographs, Kasturbai is a strikingly beautiful young woman. Gandhi said flatly that "lust" made him fascinated with her, although she was illiterate. He could not wait to go home to her after school. He decided to make her an "ideal wife" by acting like a jealous, demanding husband. She resisted his tantrums by doing as she pleased. What saved them during the early years of their marriage, he believed, was that they sometimes spent months apart for family reasons. As it turned out, Gandhi and Kasturbai, or Ba, as he called her, would be married for 62 years until her death while they were in prison.

Gandhi's school career continued to be ordinary. "My high school career was never above the average," he wrote. "I was thankful if I could pass my examinations. Distinction in the school was beyond my aspiration." But because his family hoped he would follow his father into government service, in 1887 he took the entrance examination for the University of Bombay. He passed, just barely. At the

In a marriage arranged by their families, Mohandas Gandhi wed Kasturbai (shown here) when both were 13. Though he would later rail against the practice of child marriage, his union with Kasturbai lasted 62 years, until her death.

university, he found himself struggling to understand lectures in English.

To his relief, a family friend suggested that he consider a career in law and that he study in London. Gandhi jumped at the idea of visiting, as he thought of it, "a land of philosophers and poets, the very center of civilization." The plan was expensive, however, and the Gandhi household fatherless. But after one of the brothers offered to help, Gandhi's mother reluctantly agreed, wringing a promise from her son that he would avoid alcohol, sex, and meat while in a foreign country.

In September 1888, Mohandas Gandhi, age 18, happily boarded a steamer for England. He left behind his wife, Kasturbai, and their new son, Harilal, only a few months old.

As an 18-year-old law student in London, Gandhi tried briefly to adopt the dress and manners of his English counterparts.

3

THE SHY LAWYER

ARRIVING IN LONDON in 1888, Mohandas Gandhi placed himself at the heart of the world-encircling empire ruling India. He saw first-hand its strengths, its convictions, and its shortcomings.

Great Britain, a nation cobbled out of England, Ireland, Wales, and Scotland, was proud of its successes. To be British—or, best of all, English—was enviable, the British believed, like being a Roman at the height of the Roman Empire. "The sun never sets on the British Empire" was a popular slogan of the day—a true statement because Britain controlled so many far-flung countries. Britain had reached its pinnacle of power during Queen Victoria's long reign, an exceptional era that would eventually be called the Victorian Age.

The Victorians tended to display their pride through popular books, plays, musicals, and songs. They thrilled to the adventures of detective Sherlock Holmes, for example, a typically reserved and upright English gentleman with remarkable powers of observation. Holmes appeared for the first time in Arthur Conan Doyle's novel

A Study in Scarlet, published a year before Gandhi arrived. Robert Louis Stevenson's novel *The Strange Case of Dr. Jekyll and Mr. Hyde*, set in London neighborhoods, warned readers of the chilling consequences of allowing oneself to act lawlessly and outside society. Theatergoers laughed in appreciation when musicals such as William Gilbert and Arthur Sullivan's *H.M.S. Pinafore* poked fun at typically British qualities. Even children's literature seemed bent on creating future British ladies and gentlemen. Children put themselves in the shoes of the self-reliant, unafraid heroes of Lewis Carroll's *Alice in Wonderland*, Charles Dickens's *Great Expectations*, and, in 1904, J. M. Barrie's *Peter Pan*.

Unfortunately, nothing about 18-year-old Mohandas K. Gandhi, sailing to England from Rajkot, India, was the least bit British. Soon after boarding the ship for England, he felt completely out of place. His manners were non-Western; his clothes were probably not suitable for England's cold and wet climate; and, of course, he barely spoke the language. From behind his owlish, steel-rimmed glasses, he stared out at a society in which he would be a peculiar stranger.

However, he had a questioning mind. In relocating to London, he'd unconsciously chosen the right intellectual atmosphere. His first concern upon arriving was British acceptance. He concluded that imitating the culture was the quickest way to integration. He decided to transform himself overnight from a foreign, backward bumpkin into a modern English gentleman. It would cost money, of course, which his family did not have. But he went on a spending spree anyway. He ordered new suits from the most fashionable tailors in London. He wore a showy watch on a double gold chain. He paid private tutors to teach him dancing, music, French, and, most important, how to speak and pronounce English like an educated person.

It must have come as a surprise, therefore, when he

discovered that not everyone supported or admired all Victorian values. Through friendships made in law school, he was introduced to radical thinkers on the fringe of British society. The theosophists, for instance, believed that God could only be known through spiritual self-development, not necessarily through established religious institutions such as the Catholic Church or the Anglican Church. He met anti-industrialists who criticized 19th-century advances in manufacturing and technology, arguing instead for a return to a simpler rural life, away from sprawling cities like London.

These ideas inspired Gandhi to examine his own views on life and the world. Ironically, it was in London that he first read the great Hindu poem about striving

This 1888 illustration depicts well-to-do Londoners taking a Sunday stroll in the park. In class-conscious England, Gandhi would probably never have gained complete acceptance as a Victorian gentleman. But the pull of his conscience caused him to abandon aspirations to conventional respectability anyway.

for a higher purpose, the Bhagavad Gita, or "Song of the Lord." He also studied the life and teachings of Siddhartha Gautama, better known as the Buddha, who preached that suffering resulted from craving worldly things. He read the Bible, too. According to one of his biographers, the Sermon on the Mount described in the New Testament "went straight to his heart," especially Jesus Christ's words, "But I say unto you, that ye resist not evil: but . . . . if any man will sue thee at the law and take away thy coat, let him have thy cloak also." This creed reminded him of an Indian poet, Shamal Bhatt, whose lines Gandhi had memorized as a child:

> For a bowl of water give a goodly meal;
> For a kindly greeting bow thou down with zeal;
> For a single penny pay thou back with gold;
> If the life be rescued, life do not withhold.
> Thus the words and actions of the wise regard;
> Every little service tenfold they reward.
> But the truly noble know all men as one,
> And return with gladness good for evil done.

As he continued to explore the political and philosophical issues swirling around him, Gandhi weighed in his mind such questions as how does one perform good and resist evil, how does one return love for hatred, and how does one know the nature of freedom.

After only three months in London, he dropped the pretense of becoming a cultured gentleman. It did not suit the new direction of his thinking. He began to keep track of the money he spent. He moved to less expensive rooms, cooked his own breakfast, and, to save bus fare, walked 8 to 10 miles daily. Instead of constantly pressing his family for more money, he found he could live cheaply and comfortably. As one of his biographers wrote, "Simplicity harmonized his inward and outward life; the dandyism of the first three months had been only a defensive armor against those who considered him a misfit in English society."

Then, unexpectedly, a part of his lifestyle that had earlier marked him as a misfit—his vegetarianism—actually increased his circle of friends and acquaintances.

At first, the vow he made to his mother not to eat meat caused him inconvenience and even embarrassment. During his first few weeks in London, he couldn't find enough meatless fare to provide much variety in his diet. Finally, though, he found a vegetarian restaurant. But his friends advised him that vegetarianism was foolish for several reasons—he needed red meat to keep his mind sharp; the lack of it would ruin his health; and socially, being a vegetarian was a disadvantage.

These challenges to his meatless diet, a routine he had always taken for granted, forced him to consider *why* he practiced vegetarianism. Just saying it was part of his religion, or that it was what his parents taught him, did not persuade his argumentative law-student friends.

Then he came across a pamphlet—*A Plea for Vegetarianism,* by Henry Stephens Salt—that presented a number of practical reasons for not eating meat. What especially appealed to Gandhi was that Salt cast vegetarianism as a part of social reform. First, Salt argued, eating meat raises the cost of living, even though meat is not necessary for good health. More compelling to Gandhi was that Salt, like many other vegetarians, argued that abstaining from meat and discouraging the slaughter of animals was a better moral choice. Gandhi became convinced that vegetarianism was a step toward improving oneself and society at large.

Suddenly, vegetarianism defined Gandhi's place in life better than anything else. It wasn't a pose like wearing fine clothes, speaking French, or knowing the latest dance step. It wasn't only a matter of convenience, either, as living simply was. Instead, it was part of a larger belief system that fit with other issues on his mind, including justice,

Members of the Vegetarian Society, London, 1890. As a Hindu, Gandhi (front row, right) had always abstained from eating meat, but in England he first began to see vegetarianism as a moral choice.

responsibility, and self-restraint. So he read cookbooks and learned to cook all his meals. Gradually, he eliminated rich sauces and expensive foods from his diet, relying instead on simple nourishment.

Learning to defend his stance on vegetarianism helped Gandhi overcome some of his shyness. He was good at making his case, and his friends respected him for it. He joined the executive committee of the Vegetarian Society of London and attended conferences. He also contributed nine articles to a magazine called *The Vegetarian.* This was quite an accomplishment for a young man who had once had trouble following university lectures given in English. He also met the well-known vegetarian Sir Edwin Arnold, whose books, *The Light of Asia* and *The Song Celestial,* were among Gandhi's favorites.

The pinnacle of Gandhi's London stay came when he successfully completed his studies, passed his examinations, and was called to the Bar in 1891. He was now a barrister, or lawyer, qualified to practice law in all parts of the British Empire. But self-doubts persisted. He was still rather bashful. Could he stand up in a courtroom and command attention? Even in his native India, where he planned to practice, there were brilliant and aggressive lawyers who might oppose him in a trial. So, "with just a little leaven of hope mixed with despair," as he later described his feelings, Gandhi sailed home to India.

Sad news awaited him. His mother had died only a few weeks earlier. Moreover, his family had been patient while Gandhi was in London. Now they expected a return on their emotional and financial investment. His elder brother looked forward to "wealth, and name and fame." But a law degree did not guarantee any of these things. Positions with law firms in his home state of Rajkot were scarce. In addition, Gandhi soon learned that local attorneys knew more about Indian law than he did; what's more, they charged lower fees than did their counterparts in England. Once again, Gandhi accepted the advice of family and friends, who urged him to go to Bombay to study Indian law and take any legal work he could get.

But it was even harder to compete in Bombay than in Rajkot. After a long wait, Gandhi finally landed his first case for a modest fee. Appearing in court, he rose to cross-examine a witness, but his thoughts vanished. Humiliated, he sat down again. He refunded the fee to his client and afterward fell to brooding pessimistically about his future in the practice of law.

He started grasping at straws. First, he applied for a part-time teaching position at a high school in Bombay. He was turned down. He returned to Rajkot and took a job that any experienced clerk could do—handling the paperwork for another attorney's clients. The position would have provided a regular income, except that Gandhi managed to offend a British officer of the court. The attorney fired him.

Fortunately, a job offer came in the form of a one-year, low-paying contract with a law firm in Natal, one of four provinces that the British Empire would later combine into the Union of South Africa in 1910. The terms of the contract called for him to serve as a legal adviser in a civil lawsuit. All his travel expenses would be paid. Gandhi jumped at the chance. In May 1893, he sailed for South Africa with no idea that he was stepping into a cauldron of racism.

In South Africa, Indians were nicknamed "coolies" and "fakirs." Gandhi's education in how "coolies" were treated came quickly. After landing in the port city of Durban on the eastern coast, he boarded a train for Pretoria and took a seat in the first-class section, as his ticket entitled him to do. When the train reached Pietermaritzburg late that evening, a European entered the compartment, saw Gandhi, and complained to the station manager, "Take this coolie out and put him in a lower class!" Gandhi objected—after all, he had a first-class ticket! A police-man hustled him off the train, along with his luggage. The train steamed away. Gandhi sat all night in the unlit waiting room of the Pietermaritzburg station, shivering and thinking.

His employer had failed to warn him about conditions in South Africa—was this grounds enough for breaking the contract and returning to India? And if he stayed, how would he deal with future insults? Would he accept them? During the night, Gandhi reached a decision that became the cornerstone of all his future confrontations with racism and inequality. He vowed that he would not accept injustice. He would appeal to people's better judgment through reason and protest. He felt he had no choice but to do so—not just for his own sake, but because it would be wrong to ignore one's conscience

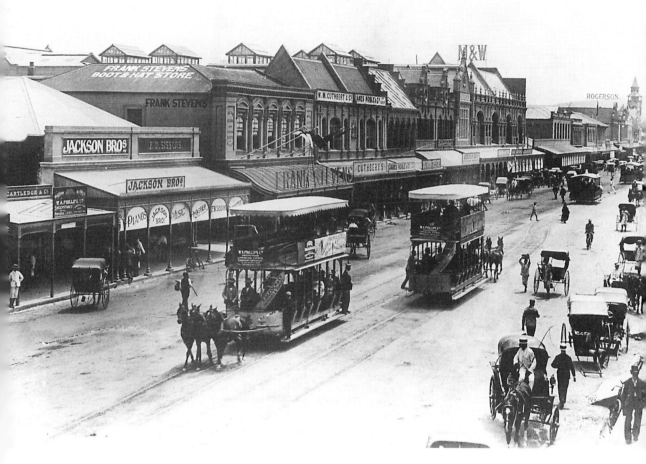

Street scene in Durban, Natal, from around the time of Gandhi's arrival in South Africa. The level of prejudice the young lawyer encountered there shocked him.

and accept mistreatment of people as a part of life. His only strategy in the fight would be truth. Later on, he coined the word *satyagraha* to describe his approach more clearly. The word comes from the Sanskrit words for "truth" and "firmness." *Satyagraha* became the basis for the type of protest most often associated with Gandhi—passive resistance and noncooperation, or peacefully refusing to comply with a rule or law because it violates one's conscience.

The next morning, Gandhi's resolve was put to the test. He boarded a train to Charlestown to continue his journey. Once there, he transferred to a stagecoach that would take him by road to Johannesburg. His employer had booked a seat for him, but the station agent cancelled Gandhi's ticket on the spot, informing him that white passengers would not ride next to a coolie. To avoid a showdown, Gandhi took a seat on the outside of the coach-box behind the coachman. Before the coach had gone very far, however, the conductor called a halt and ordered Gandhi to sit on a dirty sack on the footboard, inches from the road. Trembling, Gandhi refused. The furious conductor struck him and tried to pull him down off the coach, but Gandhi clung to a railing. Passengers came to his rescue, pleading with the conductor to stop. Gandhi resumed his seat. The coach continued on its way.

His employer in Natal was Dada Abdulla, one of the wealthiest Indian merchants in Natal. Soon after Gandhi was settled, Abdulla took him to see the court, where still another confrontation occurred. The European magistrate ordered Gandhi to take off his turban. He refused, left the courtroom, and wrote a letter of protest to the local newspaper. The news item describing the incident referred to the young lawyer from India as "an unwelcome visitor." Gandhi made use of the publicity over the issue, a tactic he would later use often. He convened a meeting of Indian residents in Pretoria to discuss their treatment in South Africa.

Despite his initial conflicts with authority, Gandhi carried out his duties as a lawyer admirably during the next year. In June 1894, he returned to Durban to depart for India. Abdulla was so pleased with Gandhi's work that he threw him a large farewell party. During the party, Gandhi happened to pick up a copy of the Natal *Mercury* newspaper and read that a bill had been introduced into the Natal legislature to disenfranchise, or deprive of equal protection under the law, all Indian settlers. Gandhi asked the other Indian merchants at the party what this would mean. They responded that they tried to stay out of politics—they were businesspeople. Gandhi countered that the connection between politics and doing business in South Africa couldn't be ignored. "This is the first nail into our coffin," he told them. Alarmed, they begged him to stay on in Natal and help them. He agreed to remain an extra month.

Instead, his one-month commitment stretched into 21 years and an apprenticeship as a leader.

Gandhi outside his law offices in South Africa, circa 1903. Though he achieved modest success as an attorney, most of his energies were devoted to the cause of civil rights for South Africa's Indian community.

4

STRUGGLE IN SOUTH AFRICA

GANDHI COULD NOT have known it when he committed an extra month to advising his friends about the bill to disenfranchise Indians, but the struggle of his fellow countrymen for basic civil rights in South Africa would be long and hard. White South Africans called all Chinese and Indian settlers "Asiatics." "The Asiatics," wrote British statesman Lord Milner, "are strangers forcing themselves upon a community reluctant to receive them." In other words, the four largest European groups in South Africa—the British, Dutch, French, and Germans—viewed the "Asiatics" as unwelcome squatters. Not even the blacks, who represented more than half of South Africa's population, received citizenship when the British government formed the Union of South Africa in 1910. The tiny "Asiatic" community, comprising as little as 2 percent of the population, was even easier to ignore.

Ironically, the Indians had come to South Africa in the first place at the urging of the whites. In the 1860s, European settlers controlled enormous tracts of virgin land in the province of Natal. These were ideal sites for tea, coffee, and sugar plantations. But the abolition of slavery meant that forced labor was no longer available. The European planters therefore sent recruiting agents around India to entice people from some of the poorest regions there to work in Natal. They offered free passage, board, and lodging; a low but steady wage; and the right to a free return passage to India after five years' "indenture," a period during which they were bound to serve or work for someone else. Immigrants would also have the option to settle in South Africa permanently, recruiters assured them. Eagerly, thousands of poor and illiterate people from the rural regions of India sailed to distant Natal.

In fact, the option to settle in Natal, or anywhere else in South Africa, was really not an opportunity the Europeans wanted Indians to seize. To discourage them, the government put roadblocks in their way. A former indentured laborer petitioning to settle in Natal had to pay a heavy tax for every member of his family. Most Indians could not afford this tax, so they lived a shadowy, illegal life. Indian merchants who followed the laborers to Natal faced additional difficulties. A license was required to do business in Natal; while Europeans could get one for free, "Asiatics" had to pay a steep fee.

These legal obstacles were less humiliating, however, than the insults routinely heaped on Indians. Disdained by whites as "Asian dirt" who lived on rice and insects, they were not permitted to walk on footpaths used by the Europeans. They could not purchase first- or even second-class tickets for transportation. European hotels and restaurants would not admit them.

This, then, was the atmosphere in the summer of 1894, when 25-year-old Mohandas Gandhi, a shy lawyer with no political experience, agreed to help his merchant friends. His goal: to defeat the bill in the Natal legislature that would further whittle away Indians' rights. Writing to

Dadabhai Naoroji, a respected member of the Indian National Congress, Gandhi expressed his willingness to help the Indian cause but also outlined his limitations as a leader: "A word for myself and what I have done. I am inexperienced and young and, therefore, quite liable to make mistakes. The responsibility undertaken is quite out of proportion to my ability. So you will see that I have not taken the matter up, which is beyond my ability, in order to enrich myself at the expense of the Indians. I am the only available person who can handle the question."

Despite doubts about his fitness to lead, Gandhi quickly succeeded in forming a community among the Natal Indians. Under his guidance, they created a small movement that attracted the attention of the South African, British, and Indian press. They circulated petitions, issued statements to the newspapers, wrote letters to influential people, and held public meetings, at which Gandhi was often the featured speaker. He also forwarded a petition with 10,000 signatures to the Colonial Office in London, protesting the proposed bill.

The bill passed anyway, but the issue of Indians' rights in South Africa had, for the first time, received wide-spread attention. Gandhi's supporters urged him to stay on in Natal. He agreed on the condition that he could earn enough as a lawyer to live comfortably in Durban. Several Indian merchants came forward and provided him with a retainer, or regular fee. In addition, he met the qualifications required to argue before the colonial Supreme Court. His career was now on solid footing.

He also realized that the Indians in Natal needed a permanent organization to champion their interests. In 1894 he formed the Natal Indian Congress, using the model of the National Congress in India, and became its secretary. The organization's purpose was to focus on issues concerning Indians.

As a first step, Gandhi urged Indians to raise their standards for education and sanitation. He argued that

Gandhi (standing, center) with the cofounders of the Natal Indian Congress, Durban, 1895.

whites would take their grievances more seriously if Indians appeared closer to the European ideals of how "civilized" people behaved. He also began bombarding friends, opponents, newspaper editors, and politicians in South Africa, Great Britain, and India with telegrams, letters, and reports on the injustices his countrymen faced. The Indian National Congress responded by lodging an official protest about the South African situation. In Britain, Gandhi's efforts caught the attention of the *London Times* newspaper, which carried several articles about the unfair treatment of British subjects from India who happened to live in another part of the empire.

Gradually, as Gandhi stepped into an increasingly larger role on the political stage, he began forming his own code about what made a politician. He decided he would not defend wrongdoing, even in the name of supporting a cause. Neither would he exaggerate just to make a point, or allow lies to pass as facts for the sake of winning. The Indian National Congress should be a reform organization, he argued, not just a means to fight politically. It should uplift Indians as well as open the eyes of their enemies to the truth.

But he could not afford to be unrealistic, either. He knew the effort to repeal discriminatory laws against Indians would take years. In 1896 he returned to India to retrieve his family and bring them to live in South Africa.

By now, Gandhi and his wife, Kasturbai, had two sons, Harilal and Manilal. Gandhi spent six months in India preparing them for the move, during which he wrote and privately printed a pamphlet that became widely read, "The Grievances of the British Indians in South Africa." Unfortunately, his words were paraphrased incorrectly in Natal newspapers, which claimed he said that Indians were "robbed and assaulted, and treated like beasts." Europeans in Natal reacted angrily to the slander. When Gandhi returned to Durban in late 1896, his enemies were waiting.

News reached Gandhi when he landed that there might be trouble. He sent Kasturbai and the boys on ahead in a carriage, setting out on foot with a friend.

"Are you the man who wrote to the press?" someone shouted, kicking him from behind.

The crowd surged toward him from all directions. Gandhi became separated from his friend as angry hands yanked off his turban, punched him, and pelted him with rocks. He feared he would be knocked unconscious, but suddenly a white woman opened her parasol to shield him. She was the police superintendent's wife. The crowd stepped back. When he learned of the incident, Joseph Chamberlain, the colonial secretary of the British cabinet, demanded that those guilty of attacking Gandhi be charged, but Gandhi refused. He said he would not rely on the courts to correct other people's behavior. His remarks won him an outpouring of support he did not expect.

The attack marked a personal turning point for Gandhi. He had been assaulted by a mob that hated him for speaking out against injustice. To counter the violence, he promoted the policy that Indians should offer passive resistance to oppression. He reasoned that the power of remaining firmly in the right—insisting nonviolently on justice and truth—was greater than the power of wrong-doers, who were forced to depend on physical abuse and intimidation to have their way. Eventually, Gandhi believed, wrongdoers would have to surrender, because injustice does not inspire people, protect them, or enlist their support. Justice, however, does. Its appeal to the human spirit is much greater, Gandhi argued. He might have pointed to his experience on the stagecoach to Johannesburg as an example of passive resistance. In that situation, he had firmly refused to move, insisting on his right to sit where he was, until the other passengers were moved to agree with him.

Gandhi's convictions about the effectiveness of passive resistance sprang in part from his reading. During his first year in South Africa, he read "quite 80 books," most of them on religion. He read the interpretations of Christianity by Russian writer Leo Tolstoy, who influenced him strongly. He also drew directly upon the teachings of Christ and on the writings of Henry David Thoreau, who argued passionately in his essay "On Civil Disobedience" about one's duty to resist wrongdoing by governments. Even so, Gandhi considered the terms *passive resistance* and *civil disobedience* too narrow for his purposes. He preferred the term he'd coined earlier, *satyagraha*, which in Sanskrit means "truth and firmness." He visited often with a group of South African Quakers, whose religious beliefs about nonviolence fit well with his. At one point, they hoped Gandhi was close to converting to Christianity, but he wasn't. He remained a Hindu throughout his life.

Meanwhile, the Gandhi family had to get on with the

business of making a new home in Durban. Kasturbai discovered that her husband's living quarters in Durban were austere. In keeping with his growing belief in the ideal of "nonpossession" as laid out in the great Hindu scripture the Bhagavad Gita, he cut his own hair and washed and ironed his own clothes. He shared his living quarters with several clerks and assistants, even though the house had no plumbing or running water. Everyone shared in the duties of running the household, including cleaning the latrine—a task usually done by "untouchables." When Kasturbai learned from her husband that she must take her turn cleaning the latrine, she was horrified. She refused, saying she would leave first. In a rage, Gandhi dragged her to the entrance gate and started to push her outside. Kasturbai pleaded that she had nowhere to go. She begged Gandhi to gain control of himself. He felt ashamed and shut the gate with Kasturbai inside.

Not long afterward, however, he insisted that Kasturbai donate all her jewels to a fund for the Indian community in Natal. Again she protested, saying she wanted them passed down in the family. But Gandhi could not be persuaded and Kasturbai surrendered every valuable "ornament," as Gandhi called them, to the poor.

Gandhi's opinions had profound effects on his eldest children, too. Having benefited little from his own education, he pulled his boys out of school, unhappy with the instruction they were receiving. He declared that he would educate them himself. But he never spent much time at it. As a result, Harilal and Manilal, says one biographer, "grew up without formal education or professional qualifications."

Gandhi also had a great deal of faith in herbal medicines and natural cures, much more than in modern medicine, and his convictions led to questionable behavior. He read a manual on obstetrics and assisted in the delivery of his third son, Ramdas, in 1897. He delivered his last son, Devadas, in 1900, entirely by himself. When Manilal came down with typhoid fever in 1902, Gandhi ignored the

Kasturbai Gandhi with her four sons, South Africa, 1902. Gandhi's failure to educate his children, particularly Harilal and Manilal, would become a source of friction later in their lives.

advice of a doctor and wrapped the boy in cold, wet sheets, then went for a walk to pray. When he returned, Manilal's fever had broken.

Gandhi was still a young man, however. His thoughts and ideas about progress and leadership were not yet fully developed. After all, no one comes into the world with a blueprint for greatness.

When the South African War, also known as the Boer War, broke out in 1899, Gandhi seems to have put his early ideas about nonviolence on hold. The war between the British and the Boers (now called Afrikaners) in the South African provinces of Natal and the Transvaal stemmed from bad feelings between the Dutch and the foreigners, most of whom were British subjects. The Boers were mainly farmers of Dutch ancestry and did not want to live under British laws.

Gandhi argued forcefully that if Indians were to claim the rights of citizens, they must support the British war effort. He organized an ambulance corps of 1,100 Indian volunteers drawn from all social levels. After undergoing training as paramedics, they tended to the wounded under fire, carrying them on stretchers to hospital tents behind the lines.

An editor for the *Pretoria News* described Gandhi after a battle: "After a night's work which had shattered men with much bigger frames, I came across Gandhi in the early morning sitting by the roadside eating a regulation biscuit. Every man in [General] Buller's force was dull and depressed, and damnation was heartily invoked on everything. But Gandhi was stoic in his bearing, cheerful and confident in his conversation and had a kindly eye."

The end of the war in 1902 saw Gandhi and his volunteers decorated for their service to the British Empire. But their sacrifice brought no change in the way Indians were treated in South Africa. In fact, just the opposite occurred, leading some of Gandhi's critics to argue that his efforts had been wasted.

In 1906 the provincial government of Transvaal issued the Asiatic Registration Bill, requiring all Indians and Chinese—men, women, and children—to register. They would be fingerprinted and issued a permit that they'd have to carry at all times. Failure to comply with this law carried penalties of fines, imprisonment, or even deportation. In addition, all marriages outside the Christian faith were considered invalid. In other words, in the eyes of the government a married Hindu couple was not officially married, and thus their children, in South Africa at least, were deemed illegitimate.

Gandhi was stunned. After 14 years of effort—petitions, letters, speeches, even his fellow Indians' willingness to serve the empire with a volunteer ambulance corps—it was clear they were no closer to equality. Perhaps they were even farther away. Speaking for all Indians, Gandhi called the bill an insult.

At a meeting in Johannesburg in September 1906, Gandhi organized a protest meeting to pledge defiance of the "Black Act," as Indians termed the bill. He stated his willingness to accept the consequences and urged passive resistance for those who would join him. In large numbers, Indians pledged not to register.

As a result, hundreds, including Gandhi, were arrested. But in court, the protesters refused to offer a defense, standing silently in defiance. When it became evident that the government could not send all the protesters to jail, it offered a compromise. The bill would be withdrawn if Indians registered voluntarily.

In February 1908 the prisoners were released. Most Indians saw the compromise as a victory, but some accused Gandhi of cowardice. As he set out to register as an example to others, an attacker struck him with a heavy stick, knocking him unconscious. "I don't want to prosecute him," said Gandhi after he revived in the home of a sympathetic Englishman. Then Gandhi arranged for a registration officer to fingerprint him as he rested.

But the government withdrew its promise. The Black Act would exist as law and would be enforced after all. Gandhi retaliated with a public bonfire of certificates. As the police moved in to disperse and arrest the 3,000 Indian protesters, Gandhi was beaten to the ground. With difficulty, he continued to reach up and throw certificates on the fire. The police dragged him off to prison.

Because many of those arrested were the sole bread-winners for their families, Gandhi, with a financial gift from a supporter, founded a communal farm for dependents in 1910. At the 1,100-acre Tolstoy Farm near Durban, work and food were shared. "We had all become laborers," Gandhi recalled later, "put on laborer's dress, but in the European style—workman's trousers and shirts that were imitated from [the] prisoner's uniform." All residents of Tolstoy Farm, including children, had to meet a quota of manual labor. Gandhi began going by the affectionate nickname Bapu, or "Father"; Kasturbai was called Ba, or "Mother."

Count Leo Tolstoy, the great Russian writer for whom the farm had been named, wrote an encouraging letter to Gandhi. "Your activity . . . is the most essential work," Tolstoy said, "the most important of all the work now being done in the world, and in which not only the nations of the Christian, but of all the world will undoubtedly take part."

By this time in his life, Gandhi was no longer the shy, inexperienced lawyer who had come to South Africa in a desperate attempt to lay the foundation of a career. Now he had entered upon the world stage as a leader, a spokesperson for the oppressed, a thinker, and a philoso-pher. One of his biographers, B. R. Nanda, described meeting him in those days:

A small, lithe, spare figure stood before me, and a refined earnest face looked into mine. The skin was dark, the eyes dark, but the smile which lighted up the face, and that

direct fearless glance, simply took one's heart by storm.
I judged him to be some thirty-eight years of age, which
proved correct. He spoke English perfectly and was
evidently a man of culture. . . . There was a quite assured
strength about him, a greatness of heart, a transparent
honesty that attracted me at once to the Indian leader.
Our Indian friend lives on a higher plane than most men
do. His actions, like the actions of Mary of Bethany, are
often counted eccentric, and not infrequently misunderstood. Those who do not know him think there is some
unworthy motive behind, some Oriental 'slimness' to
account for such profound unworldliness. But those
who know him well are ashamed of themselves in his
presence. Money, I think, has no charm for him. His
compatriots . . . wonder at him, grow angry at his strange
unselfishness, and love him with the love of pride and
trust. He is one of those outstanding characters with
whom to walk is a liberal education . . . whom to know
is to love.

For a time it seemed that the hated Black Act would be
repealed. Gopal Krishna Gokhale, an influential and
respected Indian political leader, visited South Africa to
lend support and work to negotiate a repeal of the act. But
instead, in 1913, responding to a test case, the Supreme
Court of South Africa invalidated marriages of non-
Christians in South Africa, and Gandhi launched what
turned out to be the final phase of his struggle there.

A party of 11 Indian women, including Gandhi's
wife, broke the law by crossing from the province of
Natal into the province of the Transvaal without per-
mits. Before they were arrested, they reached the coal
mines at Newcastle and pleaded with the Indian miners
to join them by striking. The miners agreed. The mine
owners retaliated by cutting off water and electricity
to areas where the miners lived. Gandhi believed he
had no choice but to take charge of the miners and

their families—2,037 men, 127 women, and 57 children.

He tried to lead them from Newcastle to Tolstoy Farm, a march of several days. He was arrested several times along the way and eventually sentenced to nine months in jail. Then the police herded the refugees onto special trains and returned them to the mines, which had been converted into prison compounds. Mounted military police forced the miners to return underground. Hearing of this, Indian miners in other parts of the country went on strike.

In 1910 Gandhi founded the communal Tolstoy Farm on 1,100 acres of land near Durban. In this photo, taken in front of one of the tents that served as living quarters, he is seated in the foreground at right.

A South African police officer confronts Gandhi, at the head of a huge column of striking miners, during the march from Newcastle to Tolstoy Farm, November 6, 1913. The miners were protesting a provision of the so-called Black Act that invalidated all non-Christian marriages.

In India, Lord Hardinge, the British viceroy, denounced as indefensible the South African government's policies toward and treatment of Indians. Under pressure from the Indian National Congress and the British Parliament, negotiations began between Gandhi and the South African government. In 1914 the tax that was charged to formerly indentured laborers who wished to become residents was abolished, marriages performed according to Indian rites were legalized, and a passport-type certificate bearing the owner's thumbprint replaced the Black Act certificate. However, Indians were still not permitted to move at will from one province to another.

Still, Gandhi considered the changes a solid victory. His struggles in South Africa confirmed his belief in the power of *satyagraha*. Just a few weeks after concluding negotiations with the South African government, he sailed for London to share the fruits of his victory with Indian leaders assembled there, including Gopal Krishna Gokhale, who had become his political mentor.

Gandhi would never return to South Africa. Instead, his journey now pointed him back to India.

Mohandas and Kasturbai Gandhi, photographed in 1915, shortly after their return to India. He had gone to South Africa as a 22-year-old, believing that he would stay there only a year. When he finally returned to his homeland, he was 44.

5

RETURN TO INDIA

WHILE GANDHI HAD been involved in the final days of the struggle for Indian rights in South Africa, Europe had been moving toward war. World War I broke out during his 1914 voyage to England. Almost as soon as he landed, on August 6, he called a meeting of his Indian friends to raise a volunteer ambulance corps like the one he'd formed during the Boer War.

Inwardly, Gandhi clung firmly to his belief in the power of nonviolence to create positive change. But he was also a strategist. The British Empire was in peril, and Gandhi believed Indians would eventually benefit if they showed their loyalty as subjects. He disagreed with those who said that Indians were slaves and should exploit Britain's crisis to fight for independence, writing later, "I did not believe that we had been quite reduced to slavery. I felt then that it was more the fault of individual British officials than of the British system, and that we could convert them by love. If we would improve our status through the help and cooperation of the British, it was our duty to win their help by standing by them in their hour of need."

The response to Gandhi's call for Indian volunteers was good, though not overwhelming. About 80 volunteers enrolled in a six-week course in paramedical training. "London in these days was a sight worth seeing," Gandhi wrote. "There was no panic, but all were busy helping to the best of their ability. Able-bodied adults began training as combatants, but what were the old, the infirm and the women to do? There was enough work for them, if they wanted. So they employed themselves in cutting and making clothes and dressings for the wounded."

Unfortunately, in the swirl of it all Gandhi contracted pleurisy, a respiratory illness, and was prevented from serving in the ambulance unit. In late 1914 he sailed to India. He would leave India only once more during his life, for a short trip to Europe in 1931.

When he stepped onto Indian soil at Bombay on January 9, 1915, Gandhi was already a national figure. The shy lawyer who had been struck speechless during his first court appearance had become a seasoned politician and widely known champion of human rights. Just days after his arrival, admirers threw a reception for him at the home of one of Bombay's leading citizens. On June 3, King Edward awarded him the Kaisar-I-Hind gold medal for public services in South Africa.

But his friend and political mentor, Gokhale, cautioned him not to jump headlong into Indian politics. He noted that Gandhi had been away for 21 years. A period of readjustment was necessary. Gandhi promised Gokhale a "year of probation," during which he would refrain from making public statements on national issues.

It was good advice. Gandhi traveled widely in India as part of his reeducation, during which he discovered, for example, that only a minority of people supported Great Britain's war effort. Many faulted him for raising an ambulance corps. In fact, only those who cared little for politics, or who worked directly for the British government, favored loyalty at all costs. He realized he had put too much emphasis on the issue of loyalty to Britain. Some interpreted it as a price they could pay now for freedom later. "That we have been loyal at a time of stress is no test of fitness for *swaraj* [self-rule]," Gandhi countered. "Loyalty is no merit. It is a necessity of citizenship all the world over."

Gandhi also spent his first year in India attending to a personal matter. A small band of friends, supporters, and relatives had followed him from South Africa. He felt obligated to help his followers in India just as he had the Newcastle coal miners. So he decided to found an *ashram,* or retreat for meditation, that would operate like Tolstoy Farm. He located it at first in Kochrab, a village near Ahmadabad, but later moved it to a better site on the bank of the river Sabarmati. He named it Satyagraha Ashram.

Gandhi once defined an ashram as "group life lived in a religious spirit." By religious, he did not mean practicing a certain faith, but following a few rules of personal conduct for spiritual self-betterment. Members of Satyagraha Ashram, for instance, vowed to uphold truth, nonviolence, and chastity. In addition, they took a second set of vows to improve conditions in India: first, to accept the untouchables (that category of people regarded as the "lowest of the low" in India); second, to do physical work, which members of India's higher castes normally refused to do; and third, to practice fearlessness in the face of oppression.

Rather than urge his followers to repeat their vows like a "Pledge of Allegiance," Gandhi called for them to be practiced in daily life. All ashram members washed their own plates and cleaned their own clothes, for example. No one served anyone else. There was a spinning and weaving room, a cowshed, and a farm where helping hands were needed. Gandhi himself could be found sweeping the grounds, or cleaning and rinsing dry beans in the kitchen. Seated at tables for evening meals were graduates of American and European universities, elderly people, Indian scholars, children, political activists, and poor farmers—all contributing in some way to the welfare of the group, regardless of their status in life. When something went wrong or people behaved badly, Gandhi, as moral and spiritual leader of the ashram, took the blame upon himself by fasting. It was a tool he used to shame people's consciences, and one he would later use to direct all of India.

He hoped that Satyagraha Ashram would become a sort of laboratory where his ideals could be put into practice for all to see. Some praised him for his vision. The Indian poet and philosopher Rabindranath Tagore, who in 1913 won the Nobel Prize for literature, called Gandhi the Mahatma, or "Great Soul," a name repeated by his admirers. Others attacked him, however, accusing him of irresponsibly defying the caste system by admitting untouchables into the ashram. To their minds, the last straw came when Gandhi adopted an untouchable girl named Lakshami. Financial support for the ashram evaporated, and Gandhi was nearly forced to close the retreat until a donor contributed a large sum of money.

Opinion in India was clearly divided over Gandhi. For one thing, his ideals and methods did not quite fit in with the two dominant political groups. The moderates did not condone his extralegal methods of *satyagraha*, which called for passive resistance. The Indian Nationalists, on the other hand, did not like his insistence on loyalty to the British government during the war. Even his motives as a leader for social change came under fire. At the urging of Gokhale, for example, Gandhi applied for admission to the Servants of India Society, a humanitarian group. But he was so controversial that debate among the society's members held up his application. When word reached Gandhi during a visit to his hometowns of Porbandar and Rajkot that Gokhale had died, Gandhi quietly withdrew his application. As a memorial to his friend and supporter, he went barefoot for a year.

Perhaps because he believed he was drawing too much attention to himself, Gandhi gradually changed the way

he dressed. During his years in South Africa, the former London dandy had dressed more and more like a working-class Indian, wearing a cap or turban, a shirt, and a *dhoti*, or long, narrow loincloth. But at one point during his travels throughout India, he decided even this was too much. A child's biography of Gandhi describes a key change in his thinking this way:

The Gandhis cut vegetables at Satyagraha Ashram. A fundamental rule of the ashram—that everyone should share in the labor—set its residents apart from the upper castes in India.

At one place, seeing the dirty clothes of women, he asked Kasturba to advise them to be clean. When Kasturba approached those women, one of them led her to her hut and said: "See, I have no other clothes. I have put on the only piece of cloth I have! How am I to wash it?" When Gandhiji heard this tale from Kasturba, he was terribly moved. . . . Henceforth he wore only a loincloth. How could he wear so many clothes, when his countrymen couldn't get the bare minimum to protect their modesty?

So he began appearing shirtless, the better to identify with the plight of the poor in India. Moreover, he began referring to himself as a weaver by trade, not an attorney, and he spent hours learning to use a spinning wheel. Later, pictures of Gandhi sitting at the spinning wheel would become a powerful symbol of his call to Indians to depend on themselves, not on the British.

Regardless of his simple dress and acts of humility, however, Gandhi still inflamed listeners with his words, especially when he spoke on the political challenges and social ills facing India. In 1916, for example, he turned a speech delivered at the dedication ceremony of Banaras Hindu University at Kashi into front-page news.

On the dais with him were the viceroy of India, Baron Chelmsford, and a number of Indian maharajas, who were beautifully arrayed in silks and jewelry. Gandhi wore laborer's clothes. When it came his turn to speak, he began in English, "It is a matter of shame that I am compelled to address my countrymen in a language that is foreign to me." Referring to other speakers who had talked about poverty in India, he continued, "You speak about the poverty of India and make an exhibition of jewelry. There is no salvation for India unless you strip yourselves of this jewelry and hold it in trust for your countrymen." He even affronted the viceroy by stating flatly, "If I find it necessary for the salvation of India that the English should be driven out, I would not hesitate to declare that they would have to go and I would be prepared to die in defense of that belief."

His remarks were both praised and condemned throughout the country. To many, he appeared to be giving mixed signals: be a good citizen, yet agitate for greater independence from Britain. Those who believed in change through constitutional means dismissed his thinking as too abstract, too lofty. India's progress toward self-rule could only be accomplished step-by-step politically, they said.

An important step toward the future of self-government and cooperation between Hindus and Moslems, for

instance, took place in December 1916. As the largest minority religion in India, Moslems wanted to make certain that the Home Rule Movement, as it was being called, took their interests into account. In December, the Indian National Congress and the All-India Moslem League agreed to the Lucknow Pact. The pact outlined how a new national-ist government of India would be organized and how Moslem and Hindu communities would operate together. Hindus agreed to give Moslems adequate representation at every major level of government. Gandhi wasn't part of the discussion—not only because he chose not to be, having recently arrived in India, but also because the Indian National Congress deliberately shut him out.

In the meantime, Gandhi occupied himself with a less sensational issue he felt was within his power to address. In December 1916 a peasant from Champaran, a village in the

At the spinning wheel, 1925. Adopting the simple dhoti, or loincloth, and going shirtless signaled Gandhi's solidarity with the poor. The spinning wheel became a potent symbol not just for individual self-sufficiency, but—because it could eliminate reliance on imported English textiles—for political independence as well.

Himalayan foothills, approached him with a complaint. The European planters forced the tenant farmers to grow indigo for dye. But despite the fact that demand for indigo had fallen off, planters were raising tenants' rents. At this rate, the farmers would soon be impoverished. Gandhi had never heard of the tiny village and knew little about the situation, but because of the farmer's persistence, he decided to investigate for himself.

All along the roads to Champaran the word spread—"He is coming!" By the time he arrived in the village, thousands of cheering people were on hand to greet him. The European district magistrate ordered Gandhi to leave, on the grounds that he was disturbing the peace. Gandhi refused and was summoned to court, where he repeated his refusal, adding, "I have disregarded the order served upon me not for want of respect for lawful authority, but in obedience to a higher law of our being, the voice of conscience." The courtroom was packed and supporters ringed the courthouse shouting slogans. The judge ordered the case postponed. Outside the courthouse, Gandhi advised the crowd to disperse. Over the next several weeks, in lawyerly fashion, he gathered evidence, took statements, and proved the case against the planters. His own case never came before the court again. It was a small initial victory for the power of *satyagraha* in India.

In March 1918 he added another personal dimension to *satyagraha*: fasting. In Ahmadabad, underpaid textile workers had launched a strike against mill owners, and the situation had reached a standoff. Gandhi pledged to fast until negotiations began. At first he feared that he'd made this commitment without thinking it through. But after only three days of his fast, strikers and mill owners came to the table for talks. The workers received a 35 percent pay increase. During the next 30 years, Gandhi would use public fasting 17 times as a means to pressure people to resolve their disputes.

Edwin Montagu, the British secretary of state for India,

provided an admiring glimpse of Gandhi and his influence during this time. In his diary, he noted that Gandhi seemed "a social reformer with a real desire to find grievances and cure them not for any reasons of self-advertisement, but to improve the conditions of his fellowmen. He dresses like a coolie, forswears all personal advancement, lives practically on the air and is a pure visionary."

Despite his showdowns with landowners and mill owners, and his stance in principle against British imperialism, Gandhi remained convinced that the British would reward Indian loyalty after the war had ended. Early in 1918, when the war took a turn for the worse for the Allies, Gandhi threw himself into recruiting Indians to volunteer as soldiers. Anti-British feelings were high, however, because the war had brought food shortages and rapid inflation. Still, Gandhi journeyed deep into the Gujarat countryside, sometimes walking 20 miles a day to reach villages when an oxcart was unavailable. The strain proved too much for him, and a severe attack of dysentery ended his campaign.

He was still recovering from his illness when Germany surrendered and the war ended. Now, he believed, he could look forward to pressing the issue of Indian self-rule with the British. With shock, he discovered that converting the British "by love" had been a foolish hope.

World War I had been the costliest war in British history, both in money and human lives lost. It had also been the most demoralizing. As a result, Great Britain was in no mood to relax its state of high alert, nor to relax its grip on India, the largest possession in its empire. In February 1919 the Rowlatt Commission recommended extending World War I emergency measures in India. Supposedly, the purpose of the measures was to control subversive activities. But Indians saw the handwriting on the wall—the British anticipated a louder demand for Indian self-rule and were moving quickly to curb civil liberties. The British government in India rushed the Rowlatt Acts through the Imperial Legislative Council in March. Gandhi listened to the eloquent protests raised in the

Indian soldiers in France during World War I. Gandhi enthusiastically recruited his countrymen to fight in Europe, believing that the British Empire would reward loyalty shown during a time of crisis. Ultimately, however, postwar British gratitude never materialized.

Indian National Congress, noting how the cries of Indian politicians fell on deaf British ears: "You can wake a man," he wrote later, "only if he is really asleep; no effort that you may make will produce any effect upon him if he is merely pretending sleep."

Although disillusioned—and roundly criticized for having advised the wrong approach with the British—Gandhi was not discouraged. He circulated a pledge of resistance to the Rowlatt Acts, describing how *satyagraha* could be used to defy them: "In the event of those bills becoming law and until they are withdrawn, we shall refuse civilly to obey these laws and such other laws as a committee to be hereafter appointed may think fit, and further affirm that in this struggle we shall faithfully follow truth and refrain from violence to life, person and property."

The acts did become law, and Home Rule leaders, continuing to agitate, were arrested. Gandhi called for a

national *hartal,* a day when all business would be suspended and people would fast and pray as a protest against
the hated legislation. Although the date for an India-wide
strike was set for April 6, 1919, a one-day strike in Delhi
on March 30 set off rioting. Local officials pleaded with
Gandhi to assist them in preventing further violence.
Gandhi set off by train for Delhi but was intercepted by
British officials and sent back to Bombay. The strike in
Bombay, as it turned out, was a complete success—the
entire city came to a standstill. But incidents of violence in
other parts of India convinced Gandhi that he had made a
"Himalayan miscalculation" in launching a mass movement of noncooperation before people understood what was
required. He returned to Satyagraha Ashram and publicly
reprimanded those who resorted to violence to combat
injustice. He fasted for three days as his way of taking
responsibility for the rioting.

Having set major events in motion, however, Gandhi
could not prevent them from reaching a tragic climax. In
the town of Amritsar in the province of the Punjab, two
local officials were arrested on April 10 for inciting civil
disobedience. On April 13 a crowd of thousands assembled
to demand their release. The demonstration gave way to
mob action. Rioters attacked two banks and killed five
Europeans. A contingent of British soldiers, under the
orders of General Dyer, trapped thousands of protesters in
an enclosed courtyard known as the Jallianwalla Bagh.
They opened fire, discharging 1,650 rounds in 10 minutes.
Four hundred people were killed and 1,200 more wounded.
The British governor of the Punjab immediately declared
martial law, giving free rein to excesses by overzealous
police, including public beatings and other humiliations,
such as making Indians crawl in the streets.

Gandhi's optimistic image of the British overlords of
India as reasonable and justice-loving crumbled before
his eyes.

A crowd of more than 100,000 Indians gathered along the banks of the Sabarmati River near Ahmadabad in April 1931 to hear Gandhi speak about independence for their country. No figure in colonial India came close to matching Gandhi's political influence and moral stature.

6

AWAKENING OF THE MASSES

AFTER THE DEATHS of hundreds in Amritsar, Gandhi hoped the British would condemn the incident as a disastrous misuse of power. Instead, the opposite happened. Rather than censuring the officers involved, some Europeans in India and abroad applauded the army's actions. Later, when the official British report on the shootings appeared, Gandhi dismissed it as a cover-up. The British Parliament held debates on the incident, but an Indian writing to Gandhi summarized the tone of the debates this way: "Our friends revealed their ignorance; our enemies their insolence."

Gandhi and his followers realized that they had been naïve to patiently expect reforms in British rule. Gestures of loyalty, citizenship, and civility, along with a willingness to negotiate, had brought no progress toward freedom. Following the bloodshed at Amritsar, Indian politicians and intellectuals called for a more radical approach, one that had been on the lips of most Indians, including Gandhi's, for decades—*swaraj* (self-rule). Rather reluctantly, Gandhi accepted that self-rule would have to be wrested from the hands of the British because they seemed unwilling to relinquish control simply because it was the right thing to do.

But he remained convinced that the best tool for achieving change was *satyagraha*—"truth and firmness." It had served him and others well on a small scale in the past. Now he believed the same principles could be used to liberate all of India while also inspiring its people to live more virtuously. For it was "not British guns, but imperfections of Indians themselves that kept their country in bondage," he maintained in his autobiography.

While the impact of Amritsar was still being felt, another strand of Indian politics suddenly made Gandhi the steward of a ready-made following. Since his return to India, he had reached out to Indian Moslems, trying to promote their interests and include them in all-India concerns. In late 1919 he was invited to a conference on an issue that had reached the boiling point with Indian Moslems—the fate of Moslem holy places in the Middle East. They worried that the victorious Allied powers would treat the sultan of Turkey harshly under the various peace treaties drafted at the end of World War I. The sultan was also the caliph, or protector of the Moslem faithful and of their holy places. It was unacceptable that the caliphate, or "Khalifat," as the Moslems spelled the word, might be reduced in its religious role.

Gandhi sat on the speakers' platform during the conference, listening to members discuss how Moslems should respond if the British government interfered with the Khalifat. As he listened, wrote one of his biographers, "Gandhi groped for a slogan. It darted into his head as spontaneously as the *hartal* idea. Non-cooperation. . . . The bad treaty would not be a law which civil resisters could break, it would be the outward and visible sign of a bad government. The right method of defying such a government was to dissociate oneself from it." Nonviolent noncooperation, Gandhi believed, could be a logical extension of *satyagraha.*

At first, Indian Moslems were unsure about such an

approach. But when terms dictated to Turkey turned out as unfavorably as they'd feared, a second conference on the issue of the Khalifat adopted nonviolent noncooperation as its official stance. Gandhi, a lifelong Hindu, found himself the head of the Khalifat movement.

He advised Moslem Indians how to practice nonviolent noncooperation. They should boycott colleges, schools, councils, and law courts; refuse to participate in activities involving British institutions; return honors granted by the British government; and resist buying foreign goods. The Indian National Congress followed suit and urged the same methods, thus launching the Non-Cooperation Movement throughout India.

The British immediately recognized that peaceful but widespread civil disobedience could wreak havoc. Lord Chelmsford, the British viceroy of India, ridiculed the whole concept, calling it "the most foolish of all schemes." Still, he noted that it would "bring ruin to those who had any stake in the country."

Noncooperation seized the imaginations of Indians, very few of whom had the means to influence the British government, but all of whom could choose not to participate in British-controlled daily life. Students deserted schools and colleges. Lawyers avoided the British courts. Parents withdrew children from British schools. Indians serving in public offices resigned. Huge bonfires consumed foreign-made goods. Sit-down protests in public places infuriated the police. Hundreds, and sometimes thousands, of protesters refused to move despite beatings and arrests.

But obviously Indians could not hope to maintain the pressure of noncooperation without creating their own resources for survival. So self-rule as a general concept evolved into two aims: economic independence and political independence. Economic independence meant breaking with two centuries of exploitation of Indian workers by British industrialists. The result of that exploitation was extreme poverty and the

Thousands of Indians took up Gandhi's call for nonviolent protests and noncooperation with the British to achieve Indian independence. Here a young volunteer blocks a cartload of imported English cloth destined for market in Bombay.

destruction of native industries such as cotton manufacturing. Gandhi urged villagers to return to simple cottage industries to support themselves. As a symbol, he began using a spinning wheel to make *khadi*, cloth made from spun yarn. "There is no beauty in the finest cloth if it makes unhappiness," he said. Clothing made of khadi became synonymous with defying foreigners—the "livery of freedom," in the words of Jawaharlal Nehru, a noncooperation leader who would later become independent India's first prime minister.

Political independence was also necessary, as Gandhi had learned firsthand in South Africa. A movement needed organized leadership, programs, and goals—especially when self-rule was the ultimate aim. Thus, Gandhi supported overhauling the constitution of the Indian National Congress. Before, the Congress had mainly been a club for the middle and upper classes. Under the revision, a pyramid design created levels of committees in the villages, districts, and provinces, ending at the top in the All-India Congress Committee and the Working Committee. In the villages he visited, Gandhi could now point to the local committees as opportunities for Indians to become politically aware and involved in bringing about change.

By the fall of 1920, Gandhi was at the center of Indian politics, with more influence than any native leader had ever had under the British. He was more than a politician, however, even more than a leader in the ordinary sense. Dressed in a loincloth, refusing material riches, calling for nonviolence or *ahimsa*—a key element of Hindu religious life—and always practicing prayer, fasting, and meditation, Gandhi became to many Indians a holy man. Biographer B. R. Nanda expressed it best: "He was loved and respected as the Mahatma, the great soul; with voluntary poverty, simplicity, humility and saintliness, he seemed a *rishi* (sage) of old who had stepped from the pages of an ancient epic to bring about the liberation of his country. Nay, to millions he was the incarnation of God. It was not only for his message that people came to him, but for the merit of seeing him. The sacred sight of the Mahatma . . . was almost equivalent to a pilgrimage to holy Banaras." The adulation was also a burden, however. Gandhi's speeches and actions were constantly discussed, second-guessed, criticized, and sometimes misunderstood. "The woes of the Mahatma are known only to the Mahatma," he wrote in a tone of weariness.

But his inspiring example drew from others a level of commitment to the Non-Cooperation Movement that wholly absorbed them. Nehru recalled in his autobiography that because of his involvement in the movement, he "gave up all other associations and contacts, old friends, books, even newspapers except in so far as they dealt with the work in hand. . . . I almost forgot my family, my wife, my daughter."

The response of the British government to the Non-Cooperation Movement was cautious at first. Lord Reading, the new viceroy who arrived in April 1921, wrote to his son, expressing how impressive Gandhi was in person. He confessed doubt, however, at whether the man's principles could influence politics. (That same year, the Indian National Congress gave Gandhi complete executive authority, with the right to name his own successor!)

Tension mounted later that year, however, when leaders of the Khalifat movement were arrested on a charge of inciting disloyalty in the army. Gandhi was arrested on a similar charge. Still later, Lord Reading met with Indian leaders, in an effort to minimize Indian insults to the Prince of Wales on his forthcoming goodwill tour. His efforts came to nothing. Everywhere the prince went that November, the streets were practically empty and the businesses shuttered. A riot broke out during his visit to Bombay. In retaliation, the British arrested noncooperation leaders and bided their time for an extreme incident that would land Gandhi himself in prison for a long time.

They did not have to wait long. Gandhi had been under pressure to orchestrate a mass civil-disobedience campaign, one that, in his words, would be "an earthquake, a sort of general upheaval on the political plane—the Government ceases to function . . . the police stations, the courts, offices, etc., all cease to be Government property and shall be taken charge of by the people." His plan was to proceed slowly, district by district, until all of India was liberated. But if violence broke out, he warned, the movement would lose its righteousness, "even as a lute would begin to emit notes of discord the moment a single string snaps."

On February 1, 1922, he informed Lord Reading in a

Lord Reading (right), who became the viceroy of India in 1921, confers with the Prince of Wales. Though he found Gandhi personally impressive, Reading doubted that the Indian leader could hold his own in the political arena. He was wrong.

letter that he would launch a campaign in Gujarat, calling on the residents to refuse to pay their taxes. Almost immediately, the protest spun out of control. Three days later, a mob in the village of Chauri Chaura attacked a police station, set it on fire, and killed 21 policemen. Gandhi reacted with a five-day fast and called off the national mass-disobedience campaign. His supporters were shocked. The entire nation was poised for action. Had he turned coward at the last moment? Lord Reading exulted to his son that Gandhi "had pretty well run himself to the last ditch as a politician."

The government made the most of the confusion following the Chauri Chaura incident. On the evening of March

10, 1922, Gandhi was arrested in his ashram on charges of sedition. The trial was held in Ahmadabad. As the British judge took his seat, he acknowledged Gandhi respectfully and said that the accused was in a different category from anyone he had ever tried. Gandhi pled guilty. The trial lasted 100 minutes, during which an observer noted that the defendant was "festively joyful." The judge sentenced him to six years in prison.

"So far as the sentence is concerned," Gandhi told the judge, "I certainly consider that it is as light as any judge would inflict on me; and so far as the whole proceedings are concerned, I must say that I could not have expected greater courtesy." Sent to Yeravada prison in Poona, Gandhi turned his sentence into, as his poet friend Rabindranath Tagore called it, an "arrest cure." He kept up his daily routine of morning and evening prayers, and spinning. He read more than 150 books and plays, including Henry James's *The Varieties of Religious Experience*, George Bernard Shaw's *Man and Superman*, H. G. Wells's *Outline of History*, Johann Wolfgang von Goethe's *Faust,* and Rudyard Kipling's *Barrack Room Ballads*. He also wrote his auto-biography, *My Experiments with Truth.*

His sentence was cut short when he suffered appendicitis. At first, he refused medical treatment but finally consented to an operation. After his recovery, popular concern over his health led to his release in 1925.

During his absence from the political scene, signs of deep cracks in Indian political life had appeared. In late 1924 Gandhi fasted for 21 days in response to Hindu-Moslem riots at Kohat, a military barracks in the Northwest Frontier. Although his fast brought both sides to the negotiating table, after his release from prison Gandhi recognized that Moslems and Hindus in India were at loggerheads. In particular, Moslems feared that Hindu domination in an independent India—should the day of liberation ever come—could leave Moslems begging for their rights. For his part, however, Gandhi never could accept that Hindus

and Moslems were two irreconcilably separate groups in Indian society.

The Indian National Congress had problems of its own, as well. The newly formed Swaraj Party declared it would seek unconditional self-rule by taking over the reins of government through elections. The No-Changers clung to the original Non-Cooperation Movement, believing that working outside the machinery of British rule would force the issue of liberation. Gandhi did his best to avoid a split. Ironically, he became the lightning rod of criticism, accused of toying with people's hopes and then backing away from a showdown with the British. The aborted mass protest in 1922 remained a sore point. Later, he defended his tactics: "The awakening of the masses was a necessary part of the training. I would do nothing to put the people to sleep again."

When a mob of Indians in the village of Chauri Chaura attacked the police station and burned to death 21 policemen in 1922, a horrified Gandhi called off the civil disobedience campaign that had just gotten under way and went on a five-day fast.

But sensing that he, rather than the destiny of India, had become a major issue in people's minds, Gandhi retired from active political life for three years. During this time, he embarked on a campaign of nation building by visiting villages all over India. Traveling by train, by oxcart, or on foot, he held the equivalent of what Americans on college campuses in the 1960s would later call "teach-ins"— informal classes held outdoors. He urged listeners to throw off destructive social customs, such as child marriage and the treatment of some people as untouchables, and he called on eligible men to marry Indian widows, who were treated poorly by Indian society. He also stressed women's equality with men. To parents who wanted only male children, a common wish that resulted in the killing of female babies, he warned, "[A]s long as we don't consider girls as natural as our boys our nation will be in a dark eclipse."

In November 1927 the British government announced the appointment of a royal commission to explore further steps toward self-government. Incredibly, the commission was careful to include representatives of the British political parties but no Indians. Outraged, the Indian National Congress decided to boycott the all-white commission "at every stage and in every form." The British secretary of state, Lord Birkenhead, turned the tables by suggesting that the Indian response confirmed England's assumption that self-rule was impractical. Stung by the insult, the Indian National Congress generated a report saying that the nation was prepared for self-government as a British dominion like Australia or Canada. But if Parliament did not accept the report by December 31, 1929, the Congress would fight for complete independence— if necessary, by resorting again to nonviolent noncooperation. Thus, Gandhi was recalled to the political arena as a guiding spirit.

The new viceroy of India, Lord Irwin, floated the possibility of dominion status in Parliament, but the concept

became the focus of long and often heated debate throughout Britain, and the government wavered. Gandhi met with Lord Irwin on December 23, 1929, to seek a solution. None came.

As a result, on the last day of the year, 40-year-old Jawaharlal Nehru, the newly appointed president of the Indian National Congress, whom Gandhi described as "pure as crystal . . . truthful beyond suspicion," unfurled a new flag representing a free India. Congress formally declared *purna swaraj*—complete independence from Britain. It called upon its members in the local legislatures to resign their seats and authorized the launching of a civil disobedience campaign.

The battle lines had been drawn.

Gandhi (shirtless, seated on the platform) meets with untouchables, 1926. His lifelong commitment to eliminating the stigma of untouchability challenged traditional Hindu customs.

With poet Sarojini Naidu during the Salt March, a 24-day trek to protest the British monopoly on salt production.

7

FREEDOM AND DIVISION

JANUARY 26, 1930, was celebrated as Independence Day throughout India. Hundreds of thousands of people took an oath that "it was a crime against man and God to submit to British rule."

Gandhi wrote later that he was "furiously thinking night and day." He believed that at last the nation was in the right mindset for a mass movement in line with the principles of *satyagraha*. Previous demonstrations had been undermined by misunderstanding and violence. What was needed was an uncomplicated but dramatic injustice that all India could protest, that even a disinterested Briton reading the *London Times* could appreciate. Gandhi found his cause in the hated salt tax.

In India, the British government enjoyed a monopoly on the production of salt. Moreover, it levied a tax on every purchase. Since salt is a staple of life, the tax fell most heavily on the poor. Gandhi asked that the tax be removed, to no avail. In March, he wrote to inform the viceroy: "On the eleventh of this month I shall proceed to break the salt law. It is open to you to arrest me. I hope there will be tens of thousands ready to take up the work after me." He announced that he would walk the 241 miles from his ashram in Ahmadabad to Dandi, a village on the Arabian Sea, and gather sea salt drying on the shore. The viceroy did not reply. In British political circles, the idea of scooping up sea salt as a way of defying the empire was ridiculed as the "kindergarten stage of political revolution."

On March 12, at 6:30 A.M., Gandhi started out from his ashram with a handful of volunteers on a march to break the salt law. As he walked, hundreds of sympathizers, as if drawn to a magnet, fell in step with the procession. At last, after 24 days, they arrived at Dandi on April 5. Gandhi spent the night in prayer. In the morning, he bathed in the sea. From the shore, he took a lump of salt, thereby breaking the salt law's prohibition against gathering salt. It was the signal for mass civil disobedience.

Word reached British officials that the Salt March included a second, more aggressive step. Gandhi planned to lead a raid on the salt warehouse at Dharsana to further prove that what was part of India rightfully belonged to Indians. He was arrested on May 5.

Two weeks later, 2,500 people assembled to carry out the raid without him. The poet Sarojini Naidu led demonstrators in prayer and appealed to them to be true *satyagrahis* and practice the spirit of Gandhi's teachings. The first wave of demonstrators advanced to the warehouse barrier erected by the British—a ditch surrounded by barbed wire. Police officers ordered the marchers to disperse. When they continued to move forward, cadres of police surged into the crowd and beat the demonstrators with bone-breaking iron truncheons.

"They went down like tenpins. From where I stood I heard the sickening whack of the clubs on unprotected skulls," a United Press correspondent wrote. A second wave of marchers followed in the footsteps of the first. Wave after wave approached the warehouse. It was reported that none of the protesters raised a hand to defend themselves. A second American newspaper correspondent at the scene

reported, "In 18 years of reporting in 22 countries, I have never witnessed such harrowing scenes as at Dharsana. Sometimes the scenes were so painful that I had to turn away momentarily. One surprising feature was the discipline of volunteers. It seemed they were thoroughly imbued with Gandhi's non-violent creed." On the first day, 2 died and 320 were injured.

Acts of organized civil disobedience broke out everywhere, from the largest cities to the smallest hamlets.

A truncheon-wielding mounted policeman disperses a crowd of demonstrators forming to raid a government salt warehouse.

Satyagrahis held meetings, observed *hartals*—days of fasting and meditation—and produced their own salt by boiling salt water in teakettles. Police beat demonstrators, arrested thousands, and even fired on crowds. The government built outdoor prisons ringed with barbed wire to hold the lawbreakers. The Indian National Congress extended the campaign by calling on protesters to gather firewood from the forests in defiance of the law, refuse to pay taxes, boycott foreign-made cloth, and sever business ties with British banks and commercial interests. The government responded by issuing emergency ordinances that suspended protesters' civil rights.

Lord Irwin, the viceroy, enforced these measures, but without enthusiasm. It was becoming clear that bringing peace in India was more important politically in Parliament and around the world than was defending Britain's unpopular and—even to the viceroy himself—increasingly immoral position. At the important British-sponsored Round Table Conference, for instance, the absence of Gandhi and his supporters left a hole in the credibility of the discussions.

So Lord Irwin ordered the release from prison of Gandhi and all members of the Indian National Congress. He and Gandhi met eight times and concluded the "Gandhi-Irwin Pact." For his part, Gandhi promised to end civil disobedience, while Lord Irwin allowed Indians living near the seacoast to make their own salt. He also released protesters from prison, granted permission for peaceful picketing, and returned confiscated property.

Nevertheless, many contemporary observers and later historians criticized the pact as a serious defeat for Gandhi. The major issues—civil rights, self-rule, whether India would be a dominion of Britain or not—were not addressed. Members of the Indian National Congress, including President Nehru, were shocked. They believed that their golden opportunity had been missed. But Gandhi remained firm in his conviction that negotiation and compromise—where before there had been only beatings and arrests—constituted a major step forward.

Gandhi may have understood just how much animosity toward him and his cause existed among old-style British empire builders. These hard-liners were outraged that the viceroy was even dealing with someone whose goal was to drive them out of India. Winston Churchill, the most prominent British political leader of the 20th century, expressed his contempt for the negotiations: "It is alarming and also nauseating to see Mr. Gandhi, a seditious Middle Temple lawyer, now posing as a fakir of a type well known in the East, striding half-naked up the steps of the Viceroy's palace while he is still organizing and conducting a defiant campaign of civil disobedience, to parley on equal terms with the representative of the King Emperor." Perhaps, then, forcing the British to negotiate at all was a victory for Gandhi, even though the British concessions merely returned India to the state that had existed *before* the mass demonstrations.

But the negotiations were not over. At the request of the Labor Party then in power in Parliament, Gandhi sailed for England in August 1931 to attend the Second Round Table Conference. He went as the sole representative of the Indian National Congress.

Here again, however, Gandhi has been faulted for making a misstep. Critics wonder where the Moslems figured in his dealings. In fact, some historians say Gandhi was prepared to give the Moslems whatever they wanted in return for their support on the issue of self-rule. But the Moslems were not directly represented by him, nor did they want to be. Many people trace the fatal split between Moslems and Hindus to Gandhi's failure to recognize that he was inflaming the Moslems by assuming too much. Then, when Moslems finally demanded their own separate state, Pakistan, carved out of India, angry Hindus accused Gandhi of failing to stand up to them. By then, of course, the damage was done.

In any case, the Second Round Table Conference was a

disappointment. Gandhi pleaded for a partnership between Great Britain and India, bound "by the silken cord of love." But already there had been a political shift in Parliament. The Conservatives who held power were more concerned about financial problems in Britain since the American stock market collapse of 1929 than about a new constitution for India. Sir Samuel Hoare, the new secretary of state, told Gandhi that he sincerely believed Indians were unfit for complete self-government.

Gandhi tried to make the best of his visit. He tramped around London in the cold wearing a white cloak and sandals. He visited the poor and met with children. The king and queen invited him to their private residence. Asked by the press whether he had been dressed well enough to meet the royal family, Gandhi joked, "The King had on enough for both of us."

But after 84 days, with nothing accomplished, he returned to India in late December 1931. In his absence, the Gandhi-Irwin Pact had fallen apart. Civil disobedience had resumed, and the Indian National Congress had been outlawed. Within a week of landing at Bombay, Gandhi was arrested and jailed. During the first nine months of 1932, the British imprisoned 61,551 Indians for civil disobedience.

Languishing in the Yeravada jail, Gandhi felt that he had to take a stand on the events occurring outside the prison walls. A proposal for a revised Indian constitution included a separate voting bloc for untouchables. Realizing that the British-supported move played on ancient prejudices and that it would permanently isolate untouchables in society, Gandhi began fasting in September in protest. His aim, as always, was not to blackmail others into seeing things his way, but to put moral pressure on them by forcing them to examine their consciences. Not long into his fast, his hope "to sting the conscience of the Hindu community into right religious action" resulted in the opening of temples to untouchables and the formation of an organization to fight the stigma of untouchability.

In London for the Second Round Table Conference on India in 1931, Gandhi received a warm, even reverent, welcome from the English people. Unfortunately, the Round Table Conference accomplished little.

Believing that real interest had now been aroused in ending untouchability, Gandhi went on a campaign after his release from prison. On November 7, 1933, he left on a nine-month, 12,500-mile countrywide tour. His efforts to wipe out the prejudice against untouchables, however, aroused the wrath of some orthodox Hindus. A bomb thrown at him in Poona injured seven, but he was unhurt. Publicly, Gandhi expressed "deep pity" for the would-be assassin.

Privately, with his keen ability to judge the popular mood, he realized that criticism of his religious approach to political and social problems was reaching a fever pitch. In October 1934, he announced his retirement from the Indian National Congress and turned instead to improving living standards in the villages where 85 percent of the Indian population lived.

During the following three years, Indian Moslems found a champion of their own in Muhammad Ali Jinnah. Born in Karachi, India—now part of Pakistan—Jinnah came from a wealthy Moslem family. In an interesting parallel to Gandhi, he studied law in England. Jinnah became famous as a lawyer in London and Bombay. In 1934 the Moslem League of India elected him its permanent president. When the Moslems did poorly in national elections several years later, Jinnah aggressively accused Indian Hindus of cooperating with the British in deliberately oppressing the Moslem minority. Moslem resentment turned an angry eye on Gandhi, in particular, for dealings with the British. Jinnah went so far as to question whether democracy would ever give Moslems in India a fair shake. In 1940, the Moslem League stated that Moslems and Hindus were two separate nations, not one. A homeland for Moslems was needed in the northern corner of the subcontinent of India.

Gandhi was stunned. To him, it was beyond understanding that the two-nation theory could be anything but an "untruth." To be an Indian meant to share a nationality, not a religion. A Bengali Moslem, he wrote, "speaks the same tongue that a Bengali Hindu does, eats the same food, has the same amusements as his Hindu neighbor. They dress alike. His [Jinnah's] name could be that of any Hindu. When I first met him, I did not know he was a Moslem."

When World War II broke out in 1939, Gandhi found himself at a moral crossroads. For 20 years, he had devoted himself to spreading the message of *satyagraha* in India as a means of resolving conflict. His earlier campaigns to raise volunteers for Britain's wars had strayed from this

Mohammed Ali Jinnah insisted on a separate state for Indian Moslems, dooming Gandhi's dream of religious tolerance in a united, independent India.

concept and resulted in nothing constructive for India. Now, perhaps sensing the seriousness of conflicts brewing between Moslems and Hindus, Gandhi clung firmly to his belief in nonviolence. He would not raise a hand to assist the international fighting and encouraged others not to do so, either. Reflecting on his earlier role in war, Gandhi wrote, "There is no defense for my conduct only in the scales of non-violence. I draw no distinction between those who wield weapons of destruction and those who do Red Cross work. Both participate in war and advance its cause. Both are guilty of the crime of war."

Gandhi's influence, coupled with Indian disenchant-
ment in general about the British, left Hindus and Moslems
alike with no enthusiasm for soldiering. Twice the British
seemed willing to discuss India's independence as a price
for volunteers: once after the fall of France in 1940, and
again after the defeat of the British in Southeast Asia in
1941. In 1942, a special emissary from London arrived to
compromise with the Indian National Congress, but the
mission failed.

At this critical time in the destiny of India, Gandhi spear-
headed the "Quit India" movement in the Indian National
Congress. Perhaps partly out of frustration over Britain's
continued reluctance to assure independence for India, and
partly out of a conviction that India would have to face
Japanese armies on its own, the Congress flatly demanded
that their centuries-old masters leave, once and for all.

The British response was severe. Gandhi, Nehru, and
most of the Indian National Congress leaders were arrested
and imprisoned. In his last speech to the Congress before his
arrest, Gandhi pleaded with Indians to stay within the
aims of nonviolent noncooperation, but his advice went
unheeded. Protests turned violent. Winston Churchill, now
prime minister of Great Britain, told the House of Commons
in Parliament that Gandhi's support "has now abandoned the
policy which Mr. Gandhi had so long inculcated in theory
and has come into the open as a revolutionary movement."
Gandhi was sentenced to internment until the end of the war.

Accompanying him to prison were Kasturbai, his wife
of over 60 years, and his personal secretary, Mahadev
Desai, who had served him for 25 years. Within a week,
Desai died. In 1944, after a long illness, Kasturbai also
died, her head resting in Gandhi's lap. When it seemed that
Gandhi might die from a malarial fever, the British, knowing the end of the war was in sight, released him, fearing
the condemnation they would suffer if he died in prison.

After his release, Gandhi tried to help break the political
deadlock over a new constitution granting self-rule to India,

but the number of players had increased to three— Hindus, Moslems, and the British. Moreover, the British were reluctant to talk about self-rule now that the emergency of World War II had ended. And, according to some sources, the Moslems under Jinnah's leadership were waiting for an opportune time to press for an independent state. At the Simla Conference in 1945, for instance, the Moslem League insisted on its right to send its own delegates, apart from the Indian National Congress, which the Congress refused to accept. Talks broke down.

In 1946 the British Parliament sent a special delegation of high-level cabinet ministers to convince the Indians of its desire to settle the self-rule issue. Negotiations bogged down on the issue of whether India would remain united, or whether the Moslems would have a separate state of Pakistan, a question that by now had become critical. Jinnah was adamant: "Let me tell you," he told the Moslem League Council in June 1946, "that Moslem India will not rest content until we have established full, complete and sovereign Pakistan."

The British suggested a complex three-tier constitution, but to no avail. The viceroy, Lord Wavell, turned to Nehru and requested that he form an interim government with which the British could deal.

So, as 1947 dawned with Hindus, Moslems, and the British at an impasse, the British prime minister, Clement Attlee, took a bold step. He announced in the House of Commons that the British government definitely intended to quit India by June 1948. If, by that date, the Indian parties did not agree on an all-India constitution, power would be transferred to "some form of Central Government in British India or in some areas to the existing Provincial Governments." Lord Mountbatten was appointed to replace Lord Wavell as Viceroy.

Lord Mountbatten arrived in India in March and invited Gandhi for a discussion. Over the next several weeks, it became clear that a partition of India was

Gandhi (near the left) visits a Moslem refugee camp, September 1947. The chaotic weeks that followed India's independence and the establishment of Pakistan saw mass migrations of Moslems and Hindus and atrocities committed by both groups. Gandhi fasted to pressure both sides to end the strife.

necessary to break the deadlock. When the issue first surfaced, the Indian National Congress had maintained that any discussion of a partition should come after liberation. But now, despite Nehru's efforts to form a closer alliance with the Moslem League, it appeared peace would come at a price, and that price was Pakistan. Gandhi countered that fear of civil war as the reason for dividing India would be a victory for violence. Talks continued between Congress leaders, the Moslem League under the guidance of Jinnah, and the British government, resulting in the Mountbatten Plan of June 3, 1947. It called for Indian independence by mid-August, and the formation of a new nation of Pakistan.

Immediately, the seismic effect of Pakistan preparing to break off from India created one of the greatest migrations in history. Moslems poured northward in caravans that wound along roads for miles. Local governments were overwhelmed by the tearing apart of communities, and violence spread.

On August 8, 1947, India declared its independence. Two days later, the Moslem state of Pakistan followed suit. Though Gandhi attended no ceremonies related to Indian independence, Nehru called him "the Father of the Nation."

But the unraveling of the bonds of nationality between Hindus and Moslems unleashed pent-up fury throughout India. Gandhi traveled everywhere, urging one thing: "the majority community must repent and make amends; the minority must forgive and make a fresh start." Civilized conduct was the duty of every individual and every community irrespective of what others did. Mountbatten called Gandhi a "one-man boundary force" between Hindus and Moslems. When riots engulfed Calcutta in September, he fasted until the combatants stopped fighting out of mutual concern for his health. Noting that the fast had accomplished what troops could not, newspapers carried the headline "The Miracle of Calcutta." In January 1948, at the age of 78, Gandhi undertook yet another fast, successfully ending Moslem-Hindu bloodshed in New Delhi.

But some Hindus were growing weary of what they saw as Gandhi's willingness to accommodate Moslems. On January 20, Nathuram Godse and several other conspirators detonated a bomb in the garden wall of Birla House in New Delhi during one of Gandhi's prayer services.

Ten days later, Godse shot Gandhi three times at close range and killed him.

The ashes of the slain Mahatma are carried through the streets of Allahabad before being placed in the sacred Ganges River.

8

GANDHI'S LEGACY

GANDHI'S DEATH WAS regarded as an international catastrophe. Numerous heads of state attended his funeral procession, and thousands of mourners dropped flower petals before the procession as it passed. The lighted funeral pyre threw brilliant flames to the sky, and afterward, as was Hindu custom, the Mahatma's ashes were cast with rose petals into the holy waters of the Ganges River.

In a prepared statement he read at his trial for Gandhi's murder, Nathuram Godse expressed his contempt for the slain leader's philosophy of nonviolence:

> Gandhi is being referred to as the Father of the Nation. But if that is so, he had failed his paternal duty inasmuch as he has acted very treacherously to the nation by his consenting to the partitioning of it. I stoutly maintain that Gandhi has failed in his duty. He has proved to be the Father of Pakistan. . . . I took courage in both my hands and I did fire the shots at Gandhiji on 30th January 1948, on the prayer-grounds of Birla House.

I do say that my shots were fired at the person whose policy and action had brought rack and ruin and destruction to millions of Hindus. . . .

I bear no ill will towards anyone individually but I do say that I had no respect for the present government owing to their policy which was unfairly favorable towards the Moslems. . . .

I now stand before the court to accept the full share of my responsibility for what I have done and the judge would, of course, pass against me such orders of sentence as may be considered proper. But I would like to add that I do not desire any mercy to be shown to me, nor do I wish that anyone else should beg for mercy on my behalf. My confidence about the moral side of my action has not been shaken even by the criticism leveled against it on all sides. I have no doubt that honest writers of history will weigh my act and find the true value thereof some day in future.

Most historians, political activists, and writers have returned more favorable judgments on the life of Gandhi. He is recognized as the driving force behind three kinds of revolutions that occurred in the 20th century: those countering colonialism, racism, and violence. During his life, Gandhi spent 2,338 days in prison in the name of causes he championed: human dignity, freedom, and nonviolence. Historical figures and movements inspired by Gandhi's life and ideas include American civil rights activists Martin Luther King Jr. and Cesar Chavez; South African political leader Nelson Mandela; and the environmental group Greenpeace and various nuclear disarmament and antiwar movements. But Gandhi himself cautioned, "There is no such thing as Gandhism and I do not want to leave any sect after me."

What, then, did he wish to demonstrate through his life's work? Primarily, he wanted people to accept nonviolence as a means of resolving conflict. Some people criticized his stance as a cover for revolution; others, as sentimental and

unrealistic. Even his supporters point out that ultimately Western parliamentary procedure led to constitutional changes in India, which in turn led to liberation.

On the other hand, the deeper principles of *satyagraha* relied on the conviction that people are neither totally good nor totally bad. Appeals to conscience can turn enemies into comrades in a common cause—the betterment of humanity. In 1931, during his visit to England, a political cartoon depicted Gandhi in a loincloth next to the fascists Benito Mussolini and Adolf Hitler, the Irish Republican Eamon De Valera, and the communist Joseph Stalin, each wearing black, brown, green, and red shirts respectively. The caption, "And he ain't wearing any bloomin' shirt

Gandhi's mortal remains were consumed by his funeral pyre in 1948, but the moral force of his life continues to inspire more than half a century later. "The light that has illumined this country for these many, many years will illumine this country for many more years," Prime Minister Nehru predicted, "and a thousand years later that light will still be seen in this country and the world will see it and it will give solace to innumerable hearts."

at all!" made the point that Gandhi did not recognize any allegiances except a moral bond that each person should share with others.

It is fair to wonder how far the rights of individuals would have advanced in South Africa and India had not Gandhi first appealed to combatants' sense of right, fairness, and compassion—their virtues, in other words, instead of their capacity for violence.

And although Gandhi has been credited with the idea of "passive resistance" through nonviolent noncooperation, his fasts, marches, speeches, and time in prison illustrate another important point: "Let me not be misunderstood. Strength does not come from physical capacity. It comes from indomitable will."

He never said important struggles for human rights would be easy or brief. But he did say that those who join in the struggle must look inward and be prepared to defend their convictions resolutely, even in the face of overwhelming oppression.

CHRONOLOGY

1869	Mohandas K. Gandhi is born on October 2 in Porbandar, India, located on the west coast of the small principality of Gujart.
1882	Marries, at 13, Kasturbai, who will be his wife until her death 62 years later.
1888	Attends law school in London, leaving behind his wife and newborn son.
1891	Is admitted to the British Bar and qualifies to practice law in all parts of the empire.
1893	Takes a one-year contract to serve as a legal adviser in South Africa.
1894	Agrees to stay on in South Africa and help his friends fight a piece of legislation that is unfair to Indians.
1899	Raises an ambulance corps of 1,100 Indian volunteers to assist the British during the Boer War.
1906	Leads protests against the Asiatic Registration Bill, which requires all Indians and Chinese to register and considers all marriages outside the Christian faith invalid.
1910	Founds Tolstoy Farm, a communal farm for displaced families of his supporters.
1913	Leads thousands of protesters on a march to Tolstoy Farm after Kasturbai and 10 other women break the law and urge coal miners to strike.
1914	Leaves South Africa permanently for India.
1918	Uses fasting as a tool of *satyagraha* to end an impasse between striking textile workers and mill owners.
1919–22	Becomes leader of the Moslem "Khalifat" movement, which evolves into the All-India Non-Cooperation Movement.
1922	Is sentenced to six years in prison; he is released in 1925.
1929	On December 31 Indian National Congress unfurls its first flag of independence.
1930	Salt March to Dandi results in massive arrests and civil disobedience.
1932	Gandhi begins campaign to end prejudice against "untouchables."
1939	Refuses to encourage enlistment on the side of the British in World War II.

1942 Spearheads the "Quit India" movement, calling on the British to leave India immediately.

1944 Wife, Kasturbai, dies in the prison cell she shared with Gandhi.

1947 Mountbatten Plan calls for the partition of India into India and Pakistan as an initial step toward liberation. On August 8, India declares its independence. Two days later, Pakistan follows suit.

1948 Gandhi is assassinated by a Hindu nationalist January 30 while attending outdoor prayer services.

FURTHER READING

Ashe, Geoffrey. *Gandhi.* New York: Stein & Day, 1968.

Brown, Judith M. *Gandhi: Prisoner of Hope.* New Haven: Yale University Press, 1989.

Dalton, Dennis. *Mahatma Gandhi: Nonviolent Power in Action.* New York: Columbia University Press, 1993.

Easwaran, Eknath. *Gandhi the Man.* Petaluma: Nilgira Press, 1978.

Ericson, Eric H. *Gandhi's Truth.* New York: Norton, 1969.

Fisher, Louis. *The Life of Mahatma Gandhi.* New York: Harper & Brothers, 1950.

Gandhi, Mohandas K. *The Story of My Experiments with Truth.* Translated by Mahadev Desai. New York: Dover Publications, 1983 reprint.

Gandhi, Rajmohan. *The Good Boatman: A Portrait of Gandhi.* New Delhi, India: Viking, 1995.

Mehta, Ved. *Mahatma Gandhi and His Apostles.* New York: The Viking Press, 1976.

Nanda, B. R. *Mahatma Gandhi.* Boston: Beacon Press, 1958.

Payne, Robert. *The Life and Death of Mahatma Gandhi.* New York: E. P. Dutton & Co., 1969.

Shirer, William Laurence. *Gandhi: A Memoir.* New York: Simon & Schuster, 1979.

Websites

Fisher, Louis. "Death Before Prayers." Haridas T. Lahari's Cyberspace *http://lahari.tripod.com/gandhi/gandhi_death.html*

"Gandhi Assassination: 'Bapu (Father) is Finished!'" (United Press Association reprint) icansay.com. *http://www.icansay.com/news/classic/classic_002.htm*

Gandhi, Arun. "Grandfather Gandhi: Peace Was His Way." M.K. Gandhi Institute for Nonviolence. *http://www.cbu.edu/Gandhi/html/grandpa_gandhi.html*

Gandhi, Mohandas K. "My Part in the War." Excerpt from *The Story of My Experiments with Truth.* Translation by Mahadev Desai. Kamat's Potpourri. *http://www.kamat.com/mmgandhi/autobio.htm*

"'Gandhi Used to Systematically Fool People. So We Killed Him.'" Interview with Gopal Godse, brother of Gandhi's assassin. Rediff on the Net. January 29, 1998. *http://www.rediff.com/news/1998/jan/29godse.htm*

"In Lord Rama Merges the Mahatma." Haridas T. Lahari's Cyberspace.
  http://lahari.tripod.com/gandhi/gandhi_death.html

Joseph, Josy. "The Room That Became Gandhi's Death." The Rediff Special.
  Haridas T. Lahari's Cyberspace.
  http://lahari.tripod.com/gandhi/gandhi_death.html

Kamat, Jyotsna. "Gandhiji and the Status of Women."
  http://www.kamat.com/mmgandhi/gandhi.htm in Kamat's Potpourri

Lal, Vinay. "Mahatma Gandhi." Manas.
  http://www.sscnet.ucla.edu/southasia/index.html

Nanda, B.R. "Gandhi: A Pictorial Biography." Institute of Advanced Studies, Nagpur, India.
  http://www.mkgandhi.org/biography/index.htm

"Profile: Mahatma Gandhi (1869-1948)." India World, Itihaas.
  http://www.itihaas.com/modern/gandhi-profile.html

Rushdie, Salman. "Mohandas Gandhi." TIME.
  http://www.time.com/time/time100/leaders/profile/gandhi.html

Tendulkar, D. G. Life of Mohandas Karamchand Gandhi. 1951. "Plassey to Amritsar."
  http://www.mahatma.org.in/BOOKS/TENDUL/tendplas.htm.

"The Story of Gandhi." Institute of Advanced Studies. Nagpur, India.
  http://www.mkgandhi.org/students/story1.htm

Wredford, Lorna. "Mahatma: Man of the Ages, Man of the Times."
  http://www.geocities.com/CapitolHill/Lobby/8522/gtxt04.html

INDEX

Charles J. Shields writes from his home near Chicago, Illinois, where he lives with his wife, Guadalupe, an elementary school principal. Shields was chairman of the English Department at Homewood-Flossmoor High School in Flossmoor, Illinois.

James Scott Brady serves on the board of trustees with the Center to Prevent Handgun Violence and is the vice chairman of the Brain Injury Foundation. Mr. Brady served as assistant to the President and White House press secretary under President Ronald Reagan. He was severely injured in an assassination attempt on the president, but remained the White House press secretary until the end of the administration. Since leaving the White House, Mr. Brady has lobbied for stronger gun laws. In November 1993, President Bill Clinton signed the Brady Bill, a national law requiring a waiting period on handgun purchases and a background check on buyers.

PICTURE CREDITS

Page

2: Hulton/Archive Photos	40: Hulton/Archive Photos	75: Hulton/Archive Photos
10: Bettmann/Corbis	44: Vithalbhai Jhaveri/ GandhiServe	77: Hulton/Archive Photos
15: Hulton/Archive Photos		79: Vithalbhai Jhaveri/ GandhiServe
16: Hulton/Archive Photos	48: Vithalbhai Jhaveri/ GandhiServe	80: Hulton/Archive Photos
18: Peter Ruhe/Archive Photos	53: Hulton/Archive Photos	83: AP/ Wide World Photos
21: Hulton/Archive Photos	54: Local History Museums/ GandhiServe	87: Popperfoto/Archive Photos
24: Vithalbhai Jhaveri/ GandhiServe		89: Hulton/Archive Photos
27: Vithalbhai Jhaveri/ GandhiServe	56: Peter Ruhe/Archive Photos	92: Corbis
	61: Vithalbhai Jhaveri/ GandhiServe	94: Hulton/Archive Photos
28: Popperfoto/Archive Photos		97: Hulton/Archive Photos
31: Hulton/Archive Photos	63: Hulton/Archive Photos	
34: Vithalbhai Jhaveri/ GandhiServe	66: Hulton-Deutsch Collections/ Corbis	Cover photo: Hulton/Archive Photos
37: Local History Museums/ GandhiServe	68: AP/ Wide World Photos	
	72: Hulton/Archive Photos	

106